PROVENCE & SOUTHEAST FRANCE

ROAD TRIPS

This edition written and researched by

**Oliver Berry, Gregor Clark, Emilie Filou,
Donna Wheeler, Nicola Williams**

HOW TO USE THIS BOOK

Reviews

In the Destinations section:

All reviews are ordered in our authors' preference, starting with their most preferred option. Additionally:

Sights are arranged in the geographic order that we suggest you visit them and, within this order, by author preference.

Eating and Sleeping reviews are ordered by price range (budget, midrange, top end) and, within these ranges, by author preference.

Symbols In This Book

✓ Top Tips		🍷 Food & Drink
🔗 Link Your Trips		🌳 Outdoors
💬 Tips from Locals		📷 Essential Photo
🚗 Trip Detour		🏃 Walking Tour
📖 History & Culture		✕ Eating
👪 Family		🛏 Sleeping

👁 Sights	🛏 Sleeping
⛱ Beaches	✕ Eating
🏃 Activities	🍷 Drinking
🎓 Courses	☆ Entertainment
☞ Tours	🛍 Shopping
✴ Festivals & Events	ℹ Information & Transport

These symbols and abbreviations give vital information for each listing:

✆ Telephone number	🐾 Pet-friendly
⏱ Opening hours	🚌 Bus
🅿 Parking	⛴ Ferry
🚭 Nonsmoking	🚊 Tram
❄ Air-conditioning	🚆 Train
@ Internet access	apt apartments
🛜 Wi-fi access	d double rooms
🏊 Swimming pool	dm dorm beds
🥗 Vegetarian selection	q quad rooms
🍴 English-language menu	r rooms
	s single rooms
👪 Family-friendly	ste suites
	tr triple rooms
	tw twin rooms

Map Legend

Routes
- Trip Route
- Trip Detour
- Linked Trip
- Walk Route
- Tollway
- Freeway
- Primary
- Secondary
- Tertiary
- Lane
- Unsealed Road
- Plaza/Mall
- Steps
- Tunnel
- Pedestrian Overpass
- Walk Track/Path

Boundaries
- International
- State/Province
- Cliff
- Wall

Population
- ✪ Capital (National)
- ◉ Capital (State/Province)
- ● City/Large Town
- ○ Town/Village

Transport
- ✈ Airport
- Cable Car/Funicular
- 🅿 Parking
- Train/Railway
- Tram
- Ⓜ Underground Train Station

Trips
- 1 Trip Numbers
- 9 Trip Stop
- Walking tour
- Trip Detour

Route Markers
- E44 E-road network
- M100 National network

Hydrography
- River/Creek
- Intermittent River
- Swamp/Mangrove
- Canal
- Water
- Dry/Salt/Intermittent Lake
- Glacier

Areas
- Beach
- Cemetery (Christian)
- Cemetery (Other)
- Park
- Forest
- Urban Area
- Sportsground

CONTENTS

House in Vaucluse

WELCOME TO
PROVENCE & SOUTHEAST FRANCE

With its shimmering coast and rustic Provençal heart, the Mediterranean south has a timeless allure. Driving here you'll travel through wildly divergent landscapes: cinematic coastline, rugged hinterland and bucolic valleys.

Southeastern France's glamorous cities, deep-blue Mediterranean and chic hilltop villages always delight. Inland, weave between fragrant lavender fields, forested gorges and Roman ruins. Linger in art galleries or be engulfed in the lush green wetlands of the Camargue.

Along the way you'll connect with the poets, painters and writers who flocked here during the 20th century, chasing sun and inspiration.

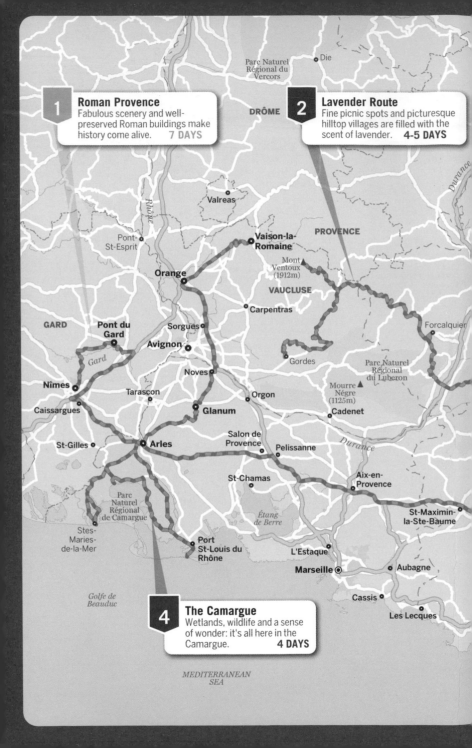

1 Roman Provence
Fabulous scenery and well-preserved Roman buildings make history come alive. **7 DAYS**

2 Lavender Route
Fine picnic spots and picturesque hilltop villages are filled with the scent of lavender. **4-5 DAYS**

4 The Camargue
Wetlands, wildlife and a sense of wonder: it's all here in the Camargue. **4 DAYS**

Parc Naturel Régional du Vercors
Die
DRÔME
Valreas
Pont-St-Esprit
Vaison-la-Romaine
PROVENCE
Orange
Mont Ventoux (1912m)
VAUCLUSE
Carpentras
GARD
Pont du Gard
Sorgues
Avignon
Gordes
Forcalquier
Gard
Noves
Parc Naturel Régional du Luberon
Nîmes
Tarascon
Orgon
Mourre Nègre (1125m)
Caissargues
Glanum
Cadenet
St-Gilles
Arles
Salon de Provence
Pelissanne
Durance
St-Chamas
Aix-en-Provence
Parc Naturel Régional de Camargue
Étang de Berre
St-Maximin-la-Ste-Baume
Stes-Maries-de-la-Mer
Port St-Louis du Rhône
L'Estaque
Marseille
Aubagne
Golfe de Beauduc
Cassis
Les Lecques
Durance
Rhône

MEDITERRANEAN SEA

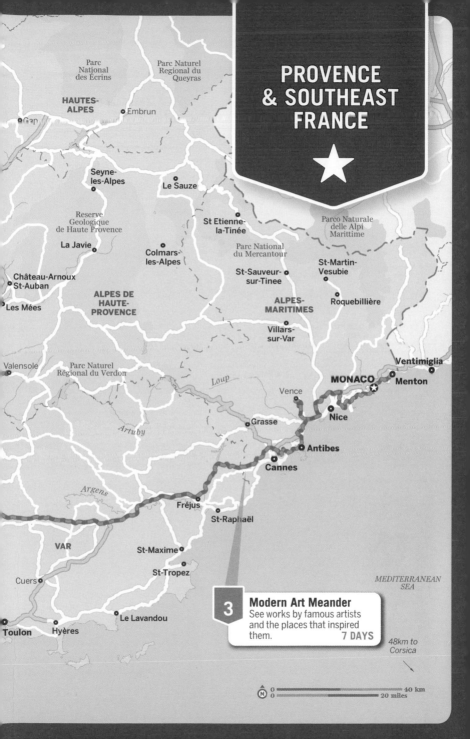

PROVENCE & SOUTHEAST FRANCE

★

Modern Art Meander

3

See works by famous artists and the places that inspired them. **7 DAYS**

PROVENCE & SOUTHEAST FRANCE HIGHLIGHTS

DANITA DELIMONT/GETTY IMAGES ©

Pont du Gard (left)
The scale of this Roman aqueduct is astonishing. View it from beside the Gard River, clamber along the top deck, or arrive after dark when it's all lit up. See it on Trip 1

Gordes (top right)
The quintessential Provençal village. See it on Trip 2

The Camargue (right)
This huge natural wetland is a paradise for nature-lovers, with its population of seabirds, wild horses and pink flamingos. See it on Trip 4

CITY GUIDE

PARIS

If ever a city needed no introduction, it's Paris – a trend setter, fashion former and style icon for centuries, and still very much at the cutting edge. Whether you're here to tick off the landmarks or seek out the secret corners, Paris fulfils all your expectations, and still leaves you wanting more.

Montmartre, Paris

Getting Around

Driving in Paris is a nightmare. Happily, there's no need for a car. The metro is fast, frequent and efficient; tickets cost €1.70 (day passes €6.70) and are valid on the city's buses. Bikes can be hired from 1800 Vélib (www.velib.paris.fr) stations; insert a credit card, authorise a €150 deposit and pedal away. Day passes cost €1; first 30 minutes free, subsequent 30 minutes from €2.

Parking

Meters don't take coins; use a chip-enabled credit card. Municipal car parks cost €2 to €3.50 an hour, or €20 to €25 per 24 hours.

Discover the Taste of Paris

Le Marais is one of the best areas for eating out, with its small restaurants and trendy bistros. Don't miss Paris' street markets: the Marché Bastille, rue Montorgueil and rue Mouffetard are full of atmosphere.

Live Like a Local

Base yourself in Montmartre for its Parisian charm, if you don't mind crowds. Le Marais and Bastille provide style on a budget, while St-Germain is good for a splurge.

Useful Websites

Paris Info (http://en.parisinfo.com) Official visitor site.

Lonely Planet (www.lonelyplanet.com/paris) Lonely Planet's city guide.

Secrets of Paris (www.secretsofparis.com) Local's blog full of insider tips.

Paris by Mouth (www.parisbymouth.com) Eat and drink your way round the capital.

TOP EXPERIENCES

➡ Eiffel Tower at Twilight
Any time is a good time to take in the panorama from the top of the 'Metal Asparagus' (as Parisians snidely call it) – but the twilight view is extra special (www.toureiffel.fr).

➡ Musée du Louvre
France's greatest repository of art, sculpture and artefacts, the Louvre is a must-visit – but don't expect to see it all in a day (www.louvre.fr).

➡ Basilique du Sacré-Coeur
Climb inside the cupola of this Montmartre landmark for one of the best cross-city vistas (www.sacre-coeur-montmartre.com).

➡ Musée d'Orsay
Paris' second-most-essential museum, with a fabulous collection encompassing originals by Cézanne, Degas, Monet, Van Gogh and more (www.musee-orsay.fr).

➡ Cathédrale de Notre-Dame
Peer over Paris from the north tower of this Gothic landmark, surrounded by gargoyles and flying buttresses (www.cathedraledeparis.com).

➡ Les Catacombes
Explore more than 2km of tunnels beneath the streets of Montparnasse, lined with the bones and skulls of millions of Parisians (www.catacombes.paris.fr).

➡ Cimetière Père-Lachaise
Oscar Wilde, Edith Piaf, Marcel Proust and Jim Morrison are just a few of the famous names buried in this wildly overgrown cemetery (www.perelachaise.com).

➡ Canal St-Martin
Join the locals for a walk or bike ride along the tow-paths of this 4.5km canal, once derelict but now reborn as a haven from the city hustle.

MATT MUNRO/LONELY PLANET ©

NICE

The classic metropolis of the French Riviera, Nice has something to suit all moods: exceptional museums, atmospheric street markets, glittering Mediterranean beaches and a rabbit-warren old town, all bathed in radiant year-round sunshine. With its blend of city grit and old-world opulence, it deserves as much time as you can spare.

Getting Around

The complicated one-way system and heavy traffic can make driving in Nice stressful, especially in the heat of summer. Walking is the easiest way to get around. There's a handy tram line from the train station all the way to Vieux Nice and place Garibaldi; tickets cost €1 and are valid on buses.

Parking

Nearly all parking in Nice is *payant* (chargeable) – assuming you manage to find a space. Car parks are usually cheapest (around €2 to €3 per hour, or €17 to €30 per day). All parking meters take coins; car-park pay stations also accept credit cards.

TOP EXPERIENCES

➡ Strolling the Promenade des Anglais
Join sun worshippers, inline skaters and dog walkers on this magnificent boulevard, which runs right along Nice's shimmering seafront.

➡ Musée Matisse
Just 2km north of the centre, this excellent art museum documents the life and work of Henri Matisse in painstaking detail. You'll need good French to get the most out of your visit (www.musee-matisse-nice.org).

➡ Shopping on Cours Saleya
This massive market captures the essence of Niçois life. A chaotic assortment of stalls sells everything from fresh-cut flowers to fresh fish.

➡ Parc du Château
Pack a picnic and head to this hilltop park for a panorama across Nice's red-tiled rooftops.

Seafront, Nice

Discover the Taste of Nice
Head for the alleyways of Vieux Nice (Old Nice) for the most authentic neighbourhood restaurants. Don't miss the local specialities of *socca* (chickpea-flour pancake), *petits farcis* (stuffed vegetables) and *pissaladière* (onion tart topped with black olives and anchovies).

Live Like a Local
Old town equals atmosphere, but for the best views and classiest rooms you'll want to base yourself near the seafront – the Promenade des Anglais has several landmark hotels. The city's cheapest hotels are clustered around the train station.

Useful Websites
Nice Tourisme (http://en.nicetourisme. com) Informative city website with info on accommodation and attractions.

Trips Through Nice: 3
Destinations coverage: p89

NEED TO KNOW

CURRENCY
Euro (€)

LANGUAGE
French

VISAS
Generally not required for stays of up to 90 days (or at all for EU nationals); some nationalities need a Schengen visa.

FUEL
Petrol stations are common around main roads and larger towns. Unleaded costs from around €1.60 per litre; *gazole* (diesel) is usually at least €0.15 cheaper.

RENTAL CARS
ADA (www.ada.fr)

Auto Europe (www.autoeurope.com)

Avis (www.avis.com)

Europcar (www.europcar.com)

Hertz (www.hertz.com)

IMPORTANT NUMBERS
Ambulance (☎15)

Police (☎17)

Fire brigade (☎18)

Europe-wide emergency (☎112)

Climate

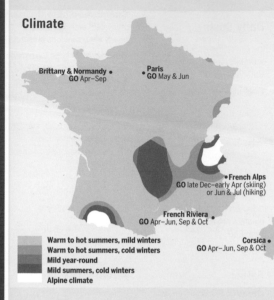

Brittany & Normandy •
GO Apr–Sep

• **Paris**
GO May & Jun

• **French Alps**
GO late Dec–early Apr (skiing) or Jun & Jul (hiking)

French Riviera •
GO Apr–Jun, Sep & Oct

Corsica •
GO Apr–Jun, Sep & Oct

Warm to hot summers, mild winters
Warm to hot summers, cold winters
Mild year-round
Mild summers, cold winters
Alpine climate

When to Go

High Season (Jul & Aug)
» The main holiday season in France – expect traffic jams and big queues, especially in August.

» Christmas, New Year and Easter are also busy times to travel.

» Late December to March is high season in French ski resorts.

Shoulder Season (Apr–Jun & Sep)
» Balmy temperatures, settled weather and light crowds make this an ideal time to travel.

» Hotel rates drop in busy areas such as southern France and the Atlantic coast.

» The *vendange* (grape harvest) happens in early autumn.

Low Season (Oct–Mar)
» Expect heavy discounts on accommodation (sometimes as much as 50%).

» Snow covers the Alps and Pyrenees, as well as much of central France.

» Many sights and hotels close down for winter.

Daily Costs

Budget: Less than €100

» Double room in a budget hotel: €50–70

» Set lunchtime *menus*: €10–15

Midrange: €100–200

» Double room in a midrange hotel: €70–120

» À la carte mains: €15–20

Top End: Over €200

» Luxury hotel room: €150–200

» Top-end restaurant meal: *menus* from €50, à la carte from €80

Eating

Cafes Coffee, drinks and bar snacks.

Bistros Serve anything from light meals to sit-down dinners.

Restaurants Range from simple *auberges* (country inns) to Michelin-starred wonders.

Vegetarians Limited choice on most menus; look out for *restaurants bios* in cities.

In this book, price symbols indicate the cost of a two-course set menu:

€	under €20
€€	€20–40
€€€	more than €40

Sleeping

Hotels France has a wide range of hotels, from budget to luxury. Unless indicated otherwise, breakfast is extra.

Chambres d'hôte The French equivalent of a B&B; prices nearly always include breakfast.

Hostels Most large towns have a hostel operated by the FUAJ (Fédération Unie des Auberges de Jeunesse).

Price symbols indicate the cost of a double room with private bathroom in high season unless otherwise noted:

€	under €80
€€	€80–100
€€€	more than €180

Arriving in France

Aéroport Roissy Charles de Gaulle (Paris)

Rental cars Major car-rental agencies have concessions at arrival terminals.

Trains, buses and RER To Paris centre every 15 to 30 minutes, 5am to 11pm.

Taxis €50 to €60; 30 minutes to Paris centre.

Aéroport d'Orly (Paris)

Rental cars Desks beside the arrivals area.

Orlyval rail, RER and buses At least every 15 minutes, 5am to 11pm.

Taxis €45 to €60; 25 minutes to Paris centre.

Mobile Phones

Most European and Australian phones work, but turn off roaming to avoid heavy data charges. Buying a French SIM card provides much cheaper call rates.

Internet Access

Wi-fi is available in most hotels and B&Bs (usually free, but sometimes for a small charge). Many cafes and restaurants also offer free wi-fi to customers.

Money

ATMs are available everywhere. Most major credit cards are accepted (with the exception of American Express). Larger cities have *bureaux de change* (exchange bureaus).

Tipping

By law, restaurant and bar prices are *service compris* (include a 15% service charge). Taxis expect around 10%; round up bar bills to the nearest euro.

Useful Websites

France Guide (www.franceguide.com) Official website run by the French tourist office.

Lonely Planet (www.lonelyplanet.com/france) Travel tips, accommodation, forum and more.

Mappy (www.mappy.fr) Online tools for mapping and journey planning.

France Meteo (www.meteo.fr) The lowdown on the French weather.

About France (www.about-france.com/travel.htm) Tips for driving in France.

For more, see Road Trip Essentials (p106)

Road Trips

Left: Menton (p37)
SYLVAIN SONNET/GETTY IMAGES ©

Roman Provence

1

Survey Provence's incredible Roman legacy as you follow ancient routes through the region's river gorges and vineyards.

TRIP HIGHLIGHTS

30 km

Pont du Gard
Aqueduct of dizzying scale, magnificently sited

Vaison-la-Romaine
FINISH

Orange **5**

175 km

Théâtre Antique
A soaring stage conjures up Rome's splendour

2

START
Nîmes **1**

St-Remy de Provence

Arles
3

95 km

Place du Forum
Bustling city square with Roman treasures below

Maison Carrée
A 1st-century-AD temple, beautiful and totally intact

0 km

7 DAYS
205KM / 127 MILES

GREAT FOR...

BEST TIME TO GO
Ruins open year-round, but avoid August's heat and crush.

ESSENTIAL PHOTO
The Pont du Gard, illuminated every night in summer.

BEST FOR CULTURE
Balmy nights at Orange's Théâtre Antique are magic; July includes the Chorégies d'Orange.

Left: Les Arènes, Nimes (p21)

1 Roman Provence

Provence was where Rome first truly flexed its imperial muscles. Follow Roman roads, cross Roman bridges and grab a seat in the bleachers at Roman theatres and arenas. Thrillingly, you'll discover that most of Provence's Roman ruins aren't ruins at all. Many are exceptionally well preserved, and some are also evocatively integrated into the modern city. With Provence's knockout landscape as a backdrop, history never looked so good!

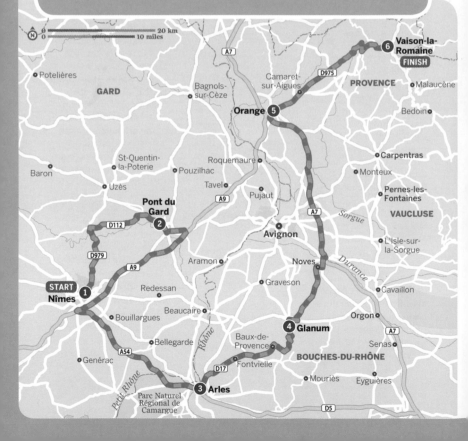

➊ Nîmes (p52)

Nîmes' bizarre coat of arms – a crocodile chained to a palm tree! – recalls the region's first, but definitely not last, horde of sun-worshipping retirees. Julius Caesar's loyal legionnaires were granted land here to settle after hard years on the Nile campaigns. Two millennia later, their ambitious town blends seamlessly with the bustling, workaday French streetscapes of the modern city. An impressively intact 1st-century-BC amphitheatre, **Les Arènes** (adult/child €9/ /; ⊙9am-6.30pm) makes for a majestic traffic roundabout. Locals nonchalantly skateboard or window-shop on the elegant place that's home to an astonishingly beautiful and preciously intact 1st-century-AD temple, the **Maison Carrée** (place de la Maison Carrée; adult/child €5.50/4; ⊙10am-8pm Jul & Aug, shorter hours rest of year). Skip the 22-minute film and instead stroll over to the elegant **Jardins de la Fontaine**. The remains of the **Temple de Diane** are in its lower northwest corner and a 10-minute uphill walk brings you to the crumbling, 30m-high **Tour Magne** (adult/child €3.40/2.90; ⊙9am-8pm Jul & Aug, shorter hours rest of

TOP TIP: PADDLING THE GARD RIVER

Get your first glimpse of the Pont du Gard from the river by paddling 8km downstream from Collias, 4km west of the D981. **Kayak Vert** (☑04 66 22 80 76; www.kayakvert.com) and **Canoë Le Tourbillon** (☑04 66 22 85 54; www.canoe-le-tourbillon.com), both based near the village bridge, rent out kayaks and canoes (€20 per person for two hours) from March/April to October.

year). Built in 15 BC as a watchtower and display of imperial grunt, it is the only one that remains of several that once spanned the 7km-long ramparts.

The Drive » The D6086 is direct, but sacrifice 15 minutes, and take route d'Uzés (D979). This way, leave Nîmes' snarly traffic behind and suddenly find yourself on a quiet stretch of winding road skirting grey rocky gorges and past honey-stone villages. Cut east via Sanilhac-Sagriès on the D112, then turn off at Begude's roundabout.

➋ Pont du Gard (p57)

You won't get a sneak peek of the **Pont du Gard** (☑04 66 37 50 99; www.pontdugard.fr; parking €18, after 8pm €10; ⊙visitor centre & museum 9am-8pm Jul & Aug, shorter hours rest of year) on approach. Nature (and clever placement of car parks and visitor centres) has created one bravura reveal. Spanning the gorge is a magnificent three-tiered aqueduct, a marvel of 1st-century

engineering. It was built around 19 BC by Agrippa, Augustus' deputy, and it's huge: the 275m-long upper tier, 48.8m above the Gard, has 35 arches. Each block (the largest weighs over 5 tonnes) was hauled in by cart or raft. It was once part of a 50km-long system that carried water from nearby Uzès down to thirsty Nîmes. It's a 400m wheelchair-accessible walk from car parks on both banks of the river to the bridge itself, with a shady cafe en route on the right. Swim upstream for unencumbered views, though downstream is also good for summer dips, with shaded wooden platforms set in the flatter banks. Want to make a day of it? There's **Musée de la Romanité**, an interactive, information-based museum, plus a children's area, and a peaceful 1.4km botanical walk, **Mémoires de Garrigue**.

The Drive » Kayaking to the next stop would be more fun, and more direct, but you'll need to hit the highway for 40 minutes to Arles – the A9 that skirts back towards Nîmes and then the A54.

TRIP HIGHLIGHT

❸ Arles (p65)

Arles, formerly known as Arelate, was part of the Roman Empire from as early as the 2nd century BC. It wasn't until the 49–45 BC civil war, however, when nearby Massalia (Marseille) supported Pompey (ie backed the wrong side), that it became a booming regional capital.

The town today is delightful, Roman cache or no, but what a living legacy it is. **Les Arènes** (Amphithéâtre; adult/child incl Théâtre Antique €6.50/5; ⊙9am-7pm) is not as larges as Nîmes', but it is spectacularly sited and occasionally still sees blood spilled, just like in the good old gladiatorial days (it hosts bullfights and *courses Camarguaises,* which is the local variation). Likewise the 1st-century **Théâtre**

Antique (☎04 90 96 93 30; bd des Lices, enter on rue de la Calade; incl Amphithéâtre admission; ⊙9am-7pm) is still regularly used for alfresco performances.

Just as social, political and religious life revolved around the forum in Arelate, the busy plane-tree-shaded **place du Forum** buzzes with cafe life today. Sip a pastis here and spot the remains of a 2nd-century temple embedded in the façade of the **Hôtel Nord-Pinus**. Under your feet are **Cryptoportiques** (place du Forum; adult/child €3.50/free; ⊙9am-noon & 2-7pm) – subterranean foundations and buried arcades. Access the underground galleries, 89m long and 59m wide, at the **Hôtel de Ville** (Town Hall; place de la République).

Emperor Constantin's partly preserved 4th-century private baths, the **Thermes de Constantin** (rue du Grand Prieuré; adult/child €3/free; ⊙9am-noon & 2-7pm), are a few minutes' stroll away, next to the quai. Southwest of the centre

is **Les Alyscamps** (adult/child €3.50/free; ⊙9am-7pm), a necropolis founded by the Romans and adopted by Christians in the 4th century. It contains the tombs of martyr St Genest and Arles' first bishops. You may recognise it: Van Gogh and Gauguin both captured the avenues of cypresses on canvas (though only melancholy old Van Gogh painted the empty sarcophagi).

The Drive ≫ Take the D17 to Fontvielle, then turn off and follow the D78F/D27A to Baux-de-Provence, then the D5. This minor detour takes you past beautiful dry white rocky hills dotted with scrubby pine; the trip will still only take around 45 minutes. There's on-site parking at Glanum. If heading into St-Rémy, there's parking by the tourist office (parking Jean-Jaurès) and north of the periphery (parking Général-de-Gaulle).

❹ Glanum (p77)

Such is the glittering allure of the gourmet delis, interiors boutiques and smart restaurants that line St-Rémy de Provence's circling boulevards and place de la République that a visit to the **Site Archéologique de Glanum** (☎04 90 92 23 79; http://glanum.monuments-nationaux.fr/en; rte des Baux-de-Provence; adult/child €7.50/free, parking €2.70; ⊙9.30am-6.30pm daily Apr-Sep, 10am-5pm Tue-Sun Oct-Mar) is often

ROMAN PROVENCE SWAT LIST

» *The Roman Provence Guide* (Edwin Mullins)

» *The Roman Remains of Southern France* (James Bromwich)

» *Southern France: An Oxford Archaeological Guide* (Henry Cleere)

» *Ancient Provence: Layers of History in Southern France* (Jeffrey Wolin)

Triumphal arch, Site Archéologique de Glanum

an afterthought. But the **triumphal arch** (AD 20) that marks Glanum's entrance, 2km south of St-Rémy, is far from insignificant. It's pegged as one of France's oldest and is joined by a towering **mausoleum** (30–20 BC). Walk down the main street and you'll pass the mainstays of Roman life: baths, a forum and marketplace, temples and town villas. And beneath all this Roman handiwork

lies the remnants of an older Celtic and Hellenic settlement, built to take advantage of a sacred spring. Van Gogh, as a patient of the neighbouring asylum, painted the olive orchard that covered the site until its excavation in the 1920s.

The Drive >> It's the A7 all the way to Orange, 50km of nondescript driving if you're not tempted by a detour to Avignon on the way.

TRIP HIGHLIGHT

⑤ Orange (p79)

It's often said if you can only see one Roman site in France, make it Orange. And yes, the town's Roman treasures are gobsmacking and unusually old; both are believed to have been built during Augustus Caesar's rule (27 BC–AD 14). Plus, while Orange may not be the Provençal village of popular fantasy, it's a cruisy, decidedly untouristy town, making for good-value accommodation and hassle-free sightseeing (such as plentiful street parking one block back from the theatre).

At a massive 103m wide and 37m high, the stage wall of the **Théâtre Antique** (www.theatre -antique.com; adult/child €9.50/7.50; ⏰9am-6pm Mar-Oct, to 4.30pm Nov-Feb) dominates the surrounding streetscape. Minus a few mosaics, plus a new roof, it's one of three in the world still standing in their entirety, and

originally seated 10,000 spectators. Admission includes an informative, if a bit overdramatic, audioguide, and access to the **Musée d'Art et d'Histoire** (☎04 90 51 17 60; museum only adult/child €5.50/4.50; ⏰9.15am-7pm summer, shorter hours in winter) across the road. Its collection includes friezes from the theatre with the Roman motifs we love: eagles holding garlands of bay leaves, and a cracking battle between cavalrymen and foot soldiers.

For bird's-eye views of the theatre – and phenomenal vistas of

rocky Mont Ventoux and the Dentelles – follow montée Philbert de Chalons, or montée Lambert, up **Colline St-Eutrope**, once the ever-vigilant Romans' lookout point.

To the town's north, the **Arc de Triomphe** stands on the ancient Via Agrippa (now the busy N7), 19m high and wide, and a stonking 8m thick. Restored in 2009, its richly animated reliefs commemorate 49 BC Roman victories with images of battles, ships, trophies, and chained, naked and utterly subdued Gauls.

SALVE, PROVINCIA GALLIA TRANSALPINA

It all starts with the Greeks. After founding the city of Massalia, now Marseille, around 600 BC, they spent the next few centuries establishing a long string of ports along the coast, planting olives and grapes as they went. When migrating Celts from the north joined forces with the local Ligurians, resistance to these booming colonies grew. The Celto-Ligurians were a force to be reckoned with; unfortunately they were about to meet ancient history's biggest bullies. In 125 BC the Romans helped the Greeks defend Massalia, and swiftly took control.

Thus begins the Gallo-Roman era and the region of Provincia Gallia Transalpina, the first Roman *provincia* (province), the name from which Provence takes it name. Later Provincia Narbonensis, it embraced all of southern France from the Alps to the Mediterranean and the Pyrenees.

Roads made the work of empire possible, and the Romans quickly set about securing a route that joined Italy and Spain. Via Aurelia linked Rome to Fréjus, Aix-en-Provence, Arles and Nîmes; the northbound Via Agrippa followed the Rhône from Arles to Avignon, Orange and onwards to Lyons. The Via Domitia linked the Alps with the Pyrenees by way of the Luberon and Nîmes.

With Julius Caesar's conquest of Gaul (58–51 BC), the region truly flourished. Under the emperor Augustus, vast amphitheatres, triumphal arches and ingenious aqueducts – the ones that propel this trip – were constructed. Augustus celebrated his final defeat of the ever-rebellious Ligurians in 14 BC, with the construction of the monument at La Turbie on the Cote d'Azur.

The Gallo-Roman legacy may be writ large and loud in Provence, but it also persists in the everyday. Look for it in unusual places: recycled into cathedral floors or hotel façades, in dusty cellars or simply buried beneath your feet.

The Drive » Northeast, the D975 passes through gentle vineyard-lined valleys for 40 minutes, with views of the Dentelles de Montmirail's limestone ridges along the way (the D977 and D23 can be equally lovely). Parking in Vaison can be a trial; nab a spot by the tourist office (place du Chanoine Saute), or try below the western walls of the Cité Médiévale, if you don't mind a walk.

⑥ Vaison-la-Romaine (p81)

Is there anything more telling of Rome's smarts than a sturdy, still-used Roman bridge? Vaison-la-Romaine's pretty little **Pont Romain** has stood the test of time and severe floods. Stand at its centre and gaze up at the walled, cobbled-street hilltop Cité Médiévale and down at the fast-flowing Ouvèze River.

Vaison-la-Romaine is tucked between seven valleys and has long been a place of trade. The ruined remains of **Vasio Vocontiorum**, the Roman city that flourished here between the 6th and 2nd centuries BC, fill two central **Gallo-Roman sites** (adult/child €8/3.50; ⊘ closed Jan). Dual neighbourhoods lie on either side of the tourist office and av du Général-de-Gaulle. The Romans shopped at the colonnaded boutiques and bathed at **La Villasse**, where you'll find **Maison au Dauphin**, which has splendid marble-lined fish ponds.

Théâtre Antique, Orange

In **Puymin**, see noblemen's houses, mosaics, a workmen's quarter, a temple and the still-functioning **Théâtre Antique** (c AD 20). To make sense of the remains (and gather your audioguide), head for the **Musée Archéologique Gallo-Roman**, which contains incredible swag – superb mosaics, carved masks and statues that include a 3rd-century silver bust and marble renderings of Hadrian and his wife, Sabina. Admission includes entry to the soothing 12th-century Romanesque cloister at **Cathédrale Notre-Dame de Nazareth** (cloister €1.50; ⊘10am-12.30pm & 2-6pm, closed Jan & Feb), a five-minute walk west of La Villasse and, like much of Provence, built on Roman foundations.

Lavender Route

2

Banish thoughts of grandma's closet. Get out among the purple haze, sniff the heady summer breezes and navigate picturesque hilltop towns, ancient churches and pretty valleys.

TRIP HIGHLIGHTS

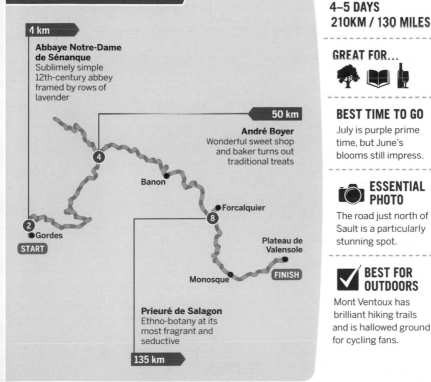

4 km

Abbaye Notre-Dame de Sénanque
Sublimely simple 12th-century abbey framed by rows of lavender

50 km

André Boyer
Wonderful sweet shop and baker turns out traditional treats

Banon

4

●**Forcalquier**

8

2
●**Gordes**

START

Plateau de Valensole

Monosque

FINISH

Prieuré de Salagon
Ethno-botany at its most fragrant and seductive

135 km

4–5 DAYS
210KM / 130 MILES

GREAT FOR...

BEST TIME TO GO
July is purple prime time, but June's blooms still impress.

ESSENTIAL PHOTO
The road just north of Sault is a particularly stunning spot.

BEST FOR OUTDOORS
Mont Ventoux has brilliant hiking trails and is hallowed ground for cycling fans.

Left: Fields of lavender, Plateau de Valensole (p33)

2 Lavender Route

The Luberon and Vaucluse may be well-trodden (and driven) destinations, but you'll be surprised at how rustic they remain. This trip takes you to the undoubtedly big-ticket (and exquisitely beautiful) sights but also gets you exploring back roads, sleepy villages, big skies and one stunner of a mountain. And yes, past fields and fields of glorious purple blooms.

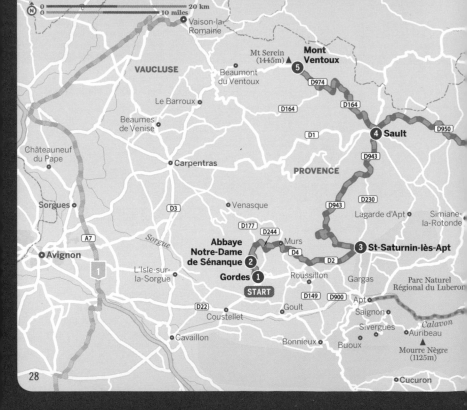

1 Gordes (p85)

The tiered village of Gordes sits spectacularly on the white-rock face of the Vaucluse plateau. It's a traditional base for those on the lavender trail, high on many tourists' must-see lists, and a favourite with posh Parisians. Gordes' star attraction is its 11th-century château, though doing laps in the cliff-side pool at the **Bastide de Gordes** can't be too bad. In truth, the thrill lies in glimpsing the village from a slight distance – come sunset, the village glows gold.

The Drive ▶ Head northwest of Gordes off the D177 with 4km of perfect Provence out your window. The descent down to the abbey is narrow, treacherous in rain, and tricky in sunshine when everyone is blinded by the lavender and pulls over. And yes, if you can, do pull over for a photograph.

TRIP HIGHLIGHT

2 Abbaye Notre-Dame de Sénanque

Isolated and ridiculously photogenic, this 12th-century Cistercian **abbey** (☎04 90 72 05 72; www.abbayedesenanque.com; adult/child €7/3; ☉9.45-11am Mon-Sat, tours by reservation) is famously framed by lavender from mid-June through July. The abbey was founded in 1148 and is still home to a small number of monks. The cloisters have a haunting, severe beauty; reservations are essential to visit inside but out of high season they can be made on-site (conservative dress and silence are required). Tours begin around 10am, so for some tranquil time with the lavender, arrive well before then.

The Drive ▶ The way out of the abbey has you heading north. Continue up the D177 then turn right onto the D244 and follow the signs to Murs, a very winding 9.5km drive accompanied by wheat fields and vineyards. From here it's about 25 minutes to the next stop.

LINK YOUR TRIP

1 Roman Provence

From Roman Provence's last stop in Vaison-la-Romaine, it's a gorgeous drive to Gordes via Carpentras and Venasque.

❸ St-Saturnin-lès-Apt (p87)

St-Saturnin-lès-Apt is a refreshingly ungentrified village, with marvellous views of the surrounding Vaucluse plateau punctuated by purple fields – climb to the **ruins** atop the village for a knockout vista. At **Moulin à Huile Jullien** (www. moulin-huile-jullien.com; rte d'Apt; ⊙ Mon-Sat) see how olives are milled into oil (with honey and oil tastings thrown in). See *lavande fine* growing at **Château du Bois** (☏ 04 90 76 91 23; www.lechateaudubois. com), a winding, but gorgeous, drive 20km to the northeast, with 80 hectares of peaceful plantings. (Note, this is a farm only; the shop and museum is in Coustellet.)

The Drive » Spot the pretty 17th-century windmill, Le Château les Moulins, 1km north, off the D943 toward Sault, then look out for the magnificent views of the red-tinged escarpment and the rust-coloured village of Roussillon. The views of Mont Ventoux only get more spectacular as you approach Sault, a 35-minute drive away.

- - - - - - - - - - -

TRIP HIGHLIGHT

❹ Sault

This drowsily charming, isolated hilltop town mixes its lavender views with plum orchards and scattered forest. Town hot spot is **André Boyer** (☏ 04 90 64 00 23; place de l'Europe), keeping farmers, cyclists and mountaineers in honey and almond nougat since 1887; its lavender marshmallows and the local speciality *pognes* (an orange-scented brioche) are also must-tries. Head to **GAEC Champelle** (☏ 04 90 64 01 50; www.gaec-champelle.fr; rte de Ventoux), a roadside farm stand northwest of town, whose products include great buys for cooks. The lavender up here is known for its dark, OK...deep purple, hue.

The Drive » This is one great 25km. Head out of town on the D164; when you hit the D974, fields give way to dense, fragrant forest (impromptu picnic, perhaps?). Above the tree line, strange spots of Alpine scrub are gradually replaced by pale bald slopes. These steep gradients have often formed a hair-raising stage of the Tour de France – the road is daubed with Tour graffiti and many fans make a brave two-wheeled homage.

- - - - - - - - - -

❺ Mont Ventoux (p82)

If fields of flowers are intoxicating, Mont Ventoux (1912m) is awe-inspiring. Nicknamed *le géant de Provence* – Provence's giant – its great white hulk is visible from much of the region. *Le géant* sparkles all year round – once the snow melts, its lunar-style limestone slopes glimmer in the sun. From its peak, clear-day vistas extend to the Alps and the Camargue.

Even summer temperatures can plummet by 20°C at the top; it's also twice as likely to rain; and the relentless mistrals blow 130 days a year, sometimes exceeding 250km/h. Bring a cardigan and scarf!

The Drive » Go back the way you came to Sault, then head east to Banon on the D950 for another 40 minutes.

TOP TIP: LAVENDER: FINDING THE GOOD OIL

When shopping for oil, the sought-after product is fine lavender (in French, *lavande fine;* in Latin, *L. officinalis*), not spike lavender (*L. latifolia*) or the hybrid lavandin (*Lavandula x intermedia*). The latter are higher in camphor; they're used in soaps and body-care products but rarely in fine perfumery. They're also used to adulterate true lavender oil. Look for oil that's clearly labelled and lacks a harsh camphor note.

Right: *Chèvre de Banon* on display, Sault

BANON
MASCARÉ
SÉCHON
CENDRÉ

❻ Banon

A tasty, nonfloral diversion: little village, big cheese. Bustling Banon is famous for its *chèvre de Banon,* a goat's-milk cheese wrapped in a chestnut leaf. Fromagerie de Banon sells its cheese at the Tuesday-morning market, and at wonderful cheese-and-sausage shop **Chez Melchio** (📞04 92 73 23 05; place de la Rèpublique; ⏰8am-7pm Jul & Aug, 8am-12.30pm & 2.30-6.30pm Wed-Sun Sep-Jun), which is unbeatable for picnic supplies. Banon's **tourist office** (📞04 92 72 19 40; www.village-banon.fr; place de la République; ⏰9am-12.30pm & 3-6pm Tue-Sat year-round, plus 10am-noon Sun Jul & Aug) has a list of *chèvre* farms you can visit. Tuck into cheese-and-charcuterie plates at **Les Vins au Vert** (📞04 92

75 23 84; www.lesvinsauvert.com; rue Pasteur; mains €12-16; ⏰ Wed-Sun); make reservations for Thursday to Saturday nights.

The Drive » Follow the D950 southeast for 25km to Forcalquier, as the scenery alternates between gentle forested slopes and fields.

❼ Forcalquier (p88)

Forcalquier has an upbeat, slightly bohemian vibe, a holdover from 1960s and '70s, when artists and back-to-the-landers arrived, fostering a now-booming organics ('*biologiques*' or bio) movement. Saffron is grown here, absinthe is distilled, and the town is also home to the L'Université Européenne des Senteurs & Saveurs (UESS; European University of Scents and Flavours). To see it all in

action, time your visit for the Monday morning market.

Climb the steep steps to Forcalquier's gold-topped **citadel** and octagonal **chapel** for more sensational views; on the way down note the once-wealthy seat's ornately carved wooden doorways and grand bourgeois town houses. Prefer to work your senses overtime? UESS' **Couvent des Cordeliers** (📞 04 92 72 50 68; www.couventdescordeliers.com) conducts workshops (€40 to €50) in perfume making, wine tasting, and aromatherapy in Forcalquier's 13th-century convent.

The Drive » Find yourself in a gentle world, all plane-tree arcades, wildflowers and, yes, lavender. Around 4km south on the D4100 you'll come to our next stop, just before the pretty town of Mane.

↱ DETOUR: THE LUBERON

Start: ❽ **Prieuré de Salagon**

The Luberon's other, southern, half is equally as florally blessed. Lavender carpets the **Plateau de Claparèdes** between **Buoux** (west), **Sivergues** (south), **Auribeau** (east) and **Saignon** (north). Cycle, walk or motor through the lavender fields and along the northern slopes of **Mourre Nègre** (1125m) – the Luberon's highest point, accessible from **Cucuron**. The D113 climbs to idyllic lavender distillery **Les Agnels** (📞04 90 74 34 60; www.lesagnels.com; rte de Buoux, btwn Buoux & Apt; free tours mid-Jul–mid-Aug), which distils lavender, cypress and rosemary. The small on-site spa has a lavender-scented swimming pool. Stay at **Chambre de Séjour avec Vue** (📞04 90 04 85 01; www.chambreavecvue.com; rue de la Bourgade; r €80-100) in tiny, hip Saignon, which perches on high rocky flanks, its narrow streets crowning a hill ringed with craggy scrub and petite lavender plots, with incredible vistas across the Luberon to Mont Ventoux.

TOP TIP: BEST PRODUCE MARKETS

The Luberon (p84) has groaning markets run from 8am to 1pm; they're particularly thrilling in summer

Monday Forcalquier

Tuesday Apt, Gordes, St-Saturnin-lès-Apt

Wednesday Gargas

Thursday Roussillon

Friday Bonnieux, Lourmarin

Saturday Apt, Manosque

Sunday Coustellet, Villars

TRIP HIGHLIGHT

8 Prieuré de Salagon (p88)

This beautiful 13th-century priory, located on the outskirts of Mane, is today home to a garden museum, the **Jardins Salagon** (04 92 75 70 50; www.musee-de-salagon.com; adult/child €7/5; 10am-8pm daily Jun-Aug, to 7pm May & Sep, to 6pm Oct–mid-Dec & Feb-Apr;). This is ethnobotany at its most poetic and sensual: wander through re-created medieval herb gardens, fragrant with native lavender, mints and mugworts. The bookshop is inviting, too.

The walled town of **Mane** is lovely for strolling. Or for a mysterious, potentially curative detour, visit remote **Église de Châteauneuf**, where a hermit church sister concocts natural remedies and makes jam. Head 800m south of Mane to the Hôtel Mas du Pont Roman, then turn right and either park and walk, or drive the bumpy final 3km. Be warned: the good sister doesn't always reveal herself. Just in case, bring a picnic and consider it an adventure.

The Drive » Get on the D13, then follow the signs to the D5, for about 30 minutes.

---

9 Manosque

Manosque has two lovely fountains and a historic cobblestoned core, but the traffic and suburban nothingness make visiting a nuisance. Why swing by? Just southeast is the home of **l'Occitane** (www.loccitane.com; Zone Industrielle St-Maurice; 10am-7pm Mon-Sat), the company that turned traditional lavender-, almond- and olive oil–based Provençal skincare into a global phenomenon. Factory tours can be booked through the **tourist office** (04 92 72 16 000); the shop offers a flat 10% discount, and the odd bargain.

The Drive » Leave the freeways and ring roads behind and cross the Durance River towards the quieter D6 (from where it will take around 20 minutes to reach the town of Valensole); make sure you check the rear-view mirrors for mountain views to the northwest as you do.

---

10 Plateau de Valensole (p88)

Things get very relaxed once you hit the D6, and the road begins a gentle climb. Picnic provisions packed, wind down your windows. This dreamily quiet plateau has Provence's greatest concentration of lavender farms, and a checkerboard of waving wheat and lavender rows stretch to the horizon, or at least until Riez. Fine picnic spots and photo ops are not hard to find.

Modern Art Meander

3

Provence is where many 20th-century artists found their greatest source of inspiration. Cross this photogenic, good-time region and discover its vibrant, creative history along the way.

TRIP HIGHLIGHTS

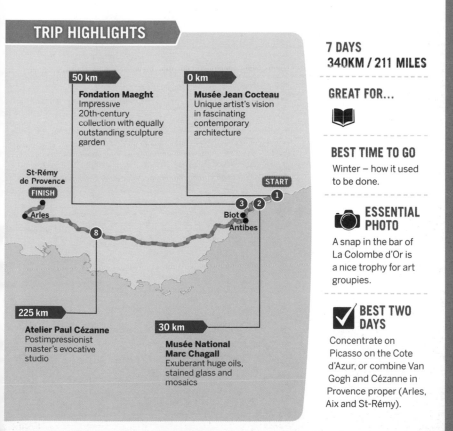

50 km

Fondation Maeght
Impressive 20th-century collection with equally outstanding sculpture garden

0 km

Musée Jean Cocteau
Unique artist's vision in fascinating contemporary architecture

St-Rémy de Provence
FINISH

Arles

START

Biot
Antibes

225 km

Atelier Paul Cézanne
Postimpressionist master's evocative studio

30 km

Musée National Marc Chagall
Exuberant huge oils, stained glass and mosaics

**7 DAYS
340KM / 211 MILES**

GREAT FOR...

BEST TIME TO GO
Winter – how it used to be done.

ESSENTIAL PHOTO
A snap in the bar of La Colombe d'Or is a nice trophy for art groupies.

BEST TWO DAYS
Concentrate on Picasso on the Cote d'Azur, or combine Van Gogh and Cézanne in Provence proper (Arles, Aix and St-Rémy).

Left: Musée Jean Cocteau Collection Séverin Wunderman (p37), Menton (Architect: Rudy Ricciotti)

35

3 Modern Art Meander

There's a particular kind of magic that happens when you connect with a work of art in the place it was created. This trip includes the region's stellar art museums, but also takes you to the bays, beaches, fields, hilltop eyries, bars and bustling boulevards where the modern masters lived, worked and partied. And it's all bathed in Provence's glorious, ever-inspirational light.

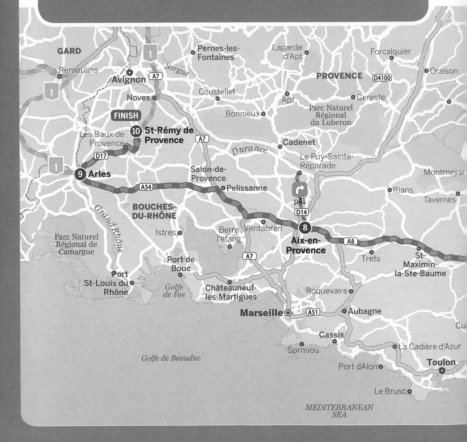

❶ Menton (p104)

Menton was once known for two things: lemons and an exceptionally sunny climate. It's now also known for its **Musée Jean Cocteau Collection Séverin Wunderman** (www.museocteaumenton. fr; 2 quai Monléon; adult/ child €6/free; ⊙10am-6pm Wed-Mon). The artist-poet Jean Cocteau was an honoured adopted son of the town; the collection focuses mainly on Cocteau's illustrations, but also includes his poetic, experimental films. You can catch delightful glimpses of palms and sparkling sea from Rudy Ricciotti's architecturally ambitious building. Cocteau decorated the local **Salle des Mariages** (Registry Office; place Ardoïno; adult/child €2/free; ⊙8.30am-noon & 2-4.30pm Mon-Fri) in 1957, and don't miss his rendering of France's official mascot, Marianne.

The Drive » Take the coast road – the gorgeous basse corniche – for about 45 minutes via Roquebrune St-Martin.

🔗 LINK YOUR TRIP

1 Roman Provence

The 20th-century artists were inspired by this heritage; join in Arles or St-Rémy (and the sunflower therapy around Nîmes is sweet).

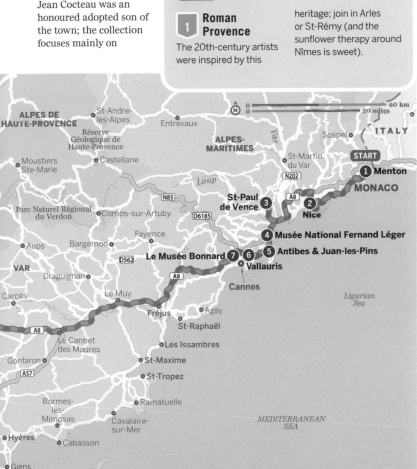

TRIP HIGHLIGHT

❷ Nice (p89)

The Cote d'Azur capital is home to two iconic museums. The **Musée National Marc Chagall** (www.musee-chagall.fr; 4 av Dr Ménard; adult/child €8/6; ☺10am-5pm Wed-Mon Oct-Jun, to 6pm Jul-Sep) houses the largest public collection of works by Marc Chagall, including monumental paintings, tapestries and glasswork. It's set in an impressive contemporary space perched high over the city. Up in the leafy quarter of Cimiez, the **Musée Matisse** (www. musee-matisse-nice.org; 164 av des Arénes de Cimiez; ☺10am-6pm Wed-Mon) overlooks an olive-tree-studded park and Roman ruins. Its beautiful Genoese villa houses a charming, if slightly underwhelming, permanent collection.

Do also make the most of Nice's burgeoning antiques and vintage scene. Browse **rue Delfy** and the streets running from place Garibaldi towards the port. The most serious dealers can be found in **rue Segurane** and the **puce** (flea market; cnr rue Robilant & quai Lunel).

The Drive » The coast road between Nice and Cannes is often gridlocked, so jump on the A8 to Cagnes-sur-Mer, about a 15-minute drive, then exit to the D336 to St-Paul de Vence. From here on, the inland run is pretty. Signs to Fondation Maeght appear 500m before the entrance to the village.

TRIP HIGHLIGHT

❸ St-Paul de Vence (p101)

Chagall, Picasso, Soutine, Léger and Cocteau 'discovered' this hilltop medieval village and were joined by the showbiz set, such as Yves Montand and Roger Moore. Chagall is buried in the **cemetery** at the village's southern end (immediately to the right as you enter).

St-Paul's fortified core is beautifully preserved but gets overrun in high summer. Escape to the **pétanque pitch**, just before the entrance to the village proper, where many a tipsy painter or tousled film star has had a spin.

Below the village, the **Fondation Maeght** (www. fondation-maeght.com; 623 chemin des Gardettes; adult/ student/child €15/9/free; ☺10am-6pm) has one of the largest private collections of 20th-century art in Europe, in a Sert-designed building that's a masterpiece itself. There's a Giacometti courtyard, sculptures dotted across the deeply terraced gardens, coloured-glass windows by Braque and mosaics by Chagall.

Head north to **Vence** and look for the blue-and-white ceramic roof tiles of Matisse's **Chapelle du Rosaire**

DIY ART COLLECTION: BROCANTE BROWSING

OK, it's highly unlikely you'll come across an obscure Picasso etching for a song. Those New York decorators and Parisian dealers will have got there first. But the *brocante* (vintage and antique) markets of Provence do continue to turn up interesting midcentury ceramics, paintings and works on paper. Banish the thought of excess baggage: these are trip mementos you'll treasure for life.

Get up early and join the locals (a regular mooch around the *puce* – flea market – is an integral part of French life), with dealers at their most charming and chatty first thing in the morning. **Isle sur La Sorgue** (an hour's drive northwest of Aix-en-Provence) is known for its sprawling stalls, and runs each weekend. Both **Nice** and **Aix-en-Provence** also have weekly meets (Nice's cours Saleya hosts on Monday mornings, Aix' on Tuesday, Thursday and Saturday on place Verdun). **Arles** holds one on the first Wednesday of the month on the bd des Lices.

(Rosary Chapel; www.vence.fr/the-rosaire-chapel.html; 466 av Henri Matisse; adult/child €6/3; ☺2-5.30pm Mon, Wed & Sat, 10-11.30am & 2-5.30pm Tue & Thu). Inside, an architecturally stark space is dominated by madly playful **stained-glass windows** in glowing blue, yellow and green, while sketchy, almost brutal, Stations of the Cross are rendered on tile; the artist declared it 'the fruit of my whole working life'.

The Drive » Head back the way you came to Cagnes, then go south for 10 minutes towards Antibes. The Musée Léger is just inland from the freeway, 2km before Biot. Look out for its brown sign.

Pottery, Vallauris

❹ Musée National Fernand Léger

Just below the charming little village of Biot, the **Musée National Fernand Léger** (www.musee-fernandleger.fr; Chemin du Val de Pòme, Biot; adult/child €5.50/free; ☺10am-6pm Tue-Sun May-Oct, to 5pm Nov-Apr) has an excellent monograph collection that captures Léger's wonderful intellectual curiosity as well as his arresting visual style.

The Drive » Head directly across the coast and then south to Antibes for about 15 minutes.

❺ Antibes & Juan-les-Pins (p103)

'If you want to see the Picassos from Antibes, you have to see them in Antibes.' So said the artist himself.

Picasso and Max Ernst were captivated by this pretty port town (as was a restless Graham Greene). Do as Picasso commanded, and head to the **Musée Picasso** (www.antibes-juanlespins.com; Château Grimaldi, 4 rue des Cordiers; adult/student/child €6/3/free; ☺10am-noon & 2-6pm Tue-Sun) in the 14th-century Château Grimaldi, his studio after WWII. Look for works featuring the serenely beautiful face of Françoise Gilot, Picasso's partner of 10 years (he met Gilot in an Antibes restaurant).

Park to explore Vieux Antibes, then hop in the car to visit **Hôtel du Cap Eden Roc**. This summer favourite of Hemingway, Picasso and others featured as the thinly disguised, fictional Hôtel des Étrangers in F Scott Fitzgerald's *Tender Is the Night* (1934).

The Drive » Take the D6107 out of Antibes, and connect with the D6007, parallel to the coast, a 20-minute trip.

❻ Vallauris

Picasso discovered this potters' village in 1947, along with his own passion for clay. He produced thousands of works here for the next eight years (many on display at the Musée Picasso in Antibes) as well as his last great political composition, a collection of dramatic murals, now part of the **Musée Picasso La Guerre et la Paix** (☎04 93 64 71 83; www.musee-picasso-vallauris. fr; place de la Libération; adult/child €3.25/free; ☻10am-noon & 2-5pm Wed-Mon). Picasso left Vallauris another gift: a dour bronze, **L'Homme au Mouton**, on place Paul Isnard (adjoining place de la Libération). But his greatest legacy was the revival of the centuries-old local ceramics industry; exuberant '60s pieces by the likes of Roger Capon are now highly collectable, and the town is today dotted with potteries.

The Drive » The D803 will get you out of Vallauris, then to the Chemin des Collines to Le Cannet, a 6km flit.

7 Le Musée Bonnard

Pierre Bonnard's luminous, quiet, intensely personal paintings are often overlooked in the fast and furious narrative of the avant-garde. Bonnard had a base in Le Cannet from 1922, and lived here almost continuously during the last decade

of his life. The collection at **Le Musée Bonnard** (☎04 93 94 06 06; www. museebonnard.fr; 16 bd Sadi Carnot, Le Cannet; adult/child/family €5/3/10; ☻10am-8pm Apr-Oct, 10am-6pm Oct-Apr) includes fascinating early pieces and ephemera, but it's the local light and colour of the artist's mature works that are truly unforgettable, for fans and new converts alike.

The Drive » Make sure you're fed and fuelled up before hitting the A8 west, with a 1½-hour drive to Aix-en-Provence. Once there, head north on the ring road, eyes peeled for the D14 exit, then veer right into the av Paul Cézanne. Note, the street is steep and there's no marked parking.

TRIP HIGHLIGHT

8 Aix-en-Provence (p59)

Oil renderings by postimpressionist Paul Cézanne of the hinterland of his hometown are forcefully beautiful and profoundly revolutionary, their use of geometric layering to create depth making way for the abstract age to come. For art lovers, Aix is hallowed ground.

TOP TIP: JEAN COCTEAU TRAIL

The dreamy work of Jean Cocteau makes a wonderful minitrip itinerary. Discover more of his Cote d'Azur legacy on the **Route Jean Cocteau** (www. le-sud-jean-cocteau.org).

The painter's last studio, **Atelier Cézanne** (www.atelier-cezanne.com; 9 av Paul Cézanne; adult/child €5.50/2; ☻10am-noon & 2-5pm), 1.5km north of town, has been painstakingly preserved. The painterly clutter is set-dressed, yes, but it's still a sublimely evocative space with soaring iron windows and sage walls washed with a patina of age. Further up the hill **Terrain des Peintres** (opposite 62 av Paul Cézanne) is a wonderful terraced garden from where Cézanne, among others, painted Montagne Ste-Victoire.

Visits to his other two sites must be booked ahead on the official **tourism website** (www. aixenprovencetourism. com): **Le Jas de Bouffan** (☎04 42 16 10 91; adult/child €5.50/2), his country manor west of the centre, and his rented cabin at **Les Carrières de Bibémus** (Bibémus Quarries; ☎04 42 16 10 91; 3090 chemin de Bibémus; adult/child €5.50/2), by a quarry on the edge of town. The latter is where he produced most of his sublime Montagne Ste-Victoire paintings.

The city's excellent **Musée Granet** (www. museegranet-aixenprovence. fr; place St-Jean de Malte; adult/child €7/free; ☻11am-7pm Tue-Sun) has nine of Cézanne's paintings, though often not on display at the same time (ironically, back in

DETOUR:
CHÂTEAU LA COSTE

Start: **8** **Aix-en-Provence**

Hello 21st century! If you're partial to site-specific installation, don't miss **Château la Coste** (☎04 42 61 92 92; www.chateau-la-coste.com; 2750 rte de la Cride, Le Puy Sainte Réparade; art walk adult/child €12/free; ⏰ art walk & wine shop 10am-7pm).

Taking a traditional domaine surrounded by wooded hills, Irish property developer Paddy McKillen has created one of the south's most compelling, and idiosyncratic, contemporary art collections. A 90-minute walk takes you out into the landscape, discovering works by artists such as Andy Goldsworthy, Sean Scully, Tatsuo Miyajima and Richard Serra. McKillen also has chosen a roll-call of starchitects to design the modern structures: a 'floating' gallery/visitors centre is by Tadeo Ando, and the cellars by Jean Nouvel. Book ahead for a guided cellar visit.

If you don't have time for the hike, taste excellent organic whites, reds and rosés in the shop, and lunch at the casual restaurant between a Louise Bourgeois spider and an Alexander Calder – bliss!

From Aix, take the D14 north. The road splits after 10km, but stay on the D14, which becomes a flawless country drive. Château la Coste is well signposted from there.

the day, the then director turned down donations by the painter himself).

The Drive » For this one-hour drive, start by getting back onto the A8 and head towards Salon-de-Provence; just before the town, take the A54 (aka E80) to Arles. Note that the N113 merges with this road from St-Martin-de-Crau.

9 Arles (p65)

Visit **Fondation Vincent Van Gogh** (☎04 90 49 94 04; www.fondation-vincentvangogh-arles.org; 33 ter rue du Docteur Fanton adult/child €9/4; ⏰11am-7pm, to 9pm Thu) to admire the contemporary architecture and design as much as for the art it showcases. The gallery hosts one or two Van Gogh–themed temporary exhibitions per year.

You can also retrace the streetscapes that fill his bursting canvases, such as the **cafe** from *Café Terrace at Night* (1888), which still sits on the place du Forum. Get a detailed Van Gogh walking map from the tourist office.

Arles today has an enduring creative vibe and a booming art and artisan scene, concentrated southwest of place du Forum and towards the *quai* (dock). It's also host to an exciting international photography festival, **Les Rencontres d'Arles Photographie** (www.rencontres-arles.com) running from early July to September.

The Drive » From Arles head to the D17. This is a 45-minute direct drive, but the Alpilles landscape is one worth slowing down for. Join the D5 after 20km

or so, then the Monastère St-Paul de Mausole is 2km before town.

10 St-Rémy de Provence (p77)

St-Rémy might be chic, but it hasn't got a Van Gogh. A couple of kilometres south of town, though, the **Monastère St-Paul de Mausole** (☎04 90 92 77 00; www.cloitresaintpaul-valetudo.com; adult/child €4.65/3.30, guided tour €8; ⏰9.30am-7pm Apr-Sep, 10.15am-5.15pm Oct-Mar) is part of the Van Gogh story, as the painter admitted himself in 1889 (he painted his *Irises* here). View a reconstruction of his room and stroll the gardens and Romanesque cloister that feature in several of his works.

The Camargue

4

Take this semicircular tour from Arles to the coast and loop back again to experience Provence at its most wild, lush and lovely. Welcome to a watery, dreamlike landscape that's like no other.

TRIP HIGHLIGHTS

35 km

Église des Stes-Maries
A 12th-century church housing the town's namesakes

START/FINISH
1

0 km

Place Paul Doumer
Possibly Provence's hippest square

Étang de Vaccarès ●
● Le Sambuc
5

3

105 km

Salin de Badon
Flamingos swoop over wetlands as you walk

Le Point ● de Vue
7

125 km

Plage de Piémanson
End-of-the-earth feel with miles of windswept beach

---

4 DAYS
190KM / 118 MILES

GREAT FOR...

BEST TIME TO GO
May, July and September – if you like it hot and can handle a mosquito or two.

ESSENTIAL PHOTO
Le Point de Vue for its salty backdrop and flocks of flamingos taking flight.

BEST FOR ROMANTICS
Dinner by the hearth in the timber-beamed 17th-century kitchen of Mas de Peint.

Left: Rue Porte de Laure, Arles (p45)

4 The Camargue

Leave Arles and the highway behind and suddenly you're surrounded by the Camargue's great yawning green, and an equally expansive sky. It won't be long until you spot your first field of cantering white horses, or face off with a black bull. This is not a long trip, but one that will plunge you into an utterly unique world of cowboys, fishermen, beachcombers, the Roma and all their enduring traditions.

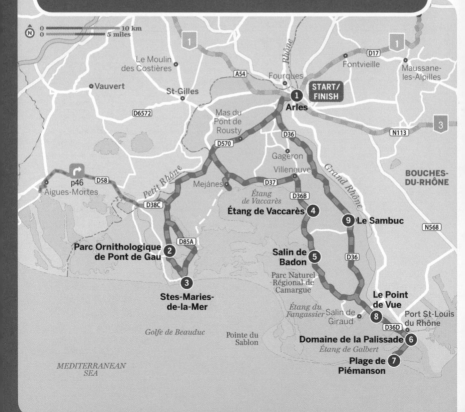

❶ Arles (p65)

Befitting its role as gateway to the Camargue, Arles has a delightfully insouciant side. Long home to bohemians of all stripes, it's a great place to hang up your sightseeing hat for a few languorous hours (or days). Soak it in from the legendary bar at the **Hôtel Nord-Pinus**, with its bullfighting trophies and enthralling photography collection, or pull up a table on lively **place Paul Doumer**, where Arles' new generation makes its mark. Make a beeline for Saturday-morning's **market** (bd des Lices) and pack a Camargue-worthy picnic basket with local goats' cheese, olives and *saucisson d'Arles* (bull-meat sausage), or do likewise on Wednesday

LINK YOUR TRIP

1 Roman Provence

Slot in the Camargue trip's loop south from either Nîmes or Arles.

3 Modern Art Meander

Need some culture after all this nature? Start in Arles.

mornings on bd Émile Combes.

With precious little parking within the old town, unless you're staying at a hotel with a garage (usually an expensive extra), opt for the secure municipal facilities on bd des Lices (€7 per day).

The Drive » Take the D35A across the Grand Rhône at the Pont de Trinquetaille, then follow signs to the D570 – you'll soon be in no doubt you've entered the Camargue. Continue south on the D570 until Pont de Gau, 4km before you hit the coast, around 30 minutes all up.

❷ Parc Ornithologique de Pont de Gau

Itching to get in among all that green? **Parc Ornithologique de Pont de Gau** ([☎]04 90 97 82 62; www.parcornithologique. com; Pont de Gau; adult/child €7.50/5; [🕙]9am-sunset Apr-Sep, from 10am rest of year), a 60-hectare bird park, makes for a perfect pit stop. As you meander along 7km of trails, flamingos pirouette overhead; while the pink birds can't help play diva, the marshes here also secret every bird species that call the Camargue wetlands home, including herons, storks, egrets, teals and raptors.

The Drive » Continue south on the D570. The last stretch of road into Stes-Maries-de-la-Mer is dotted with stables – little-

white-horse heaven, so get out your camera.

❸ Stes-Maries-de-la-Mer (p74)

Apart from a stretch of fine sand beaches – some 30km – the main attraction at this rough-and-tumble beach resort is the hauntingly beautiful **Église des Stes-Maries** (place Jean XXIII), a 12th-century church that's home to a statue of Sara-la-Kali, or black Sara. The crypt houses her alleged remains, along with those of Marie-Salomé and Sainte Marie-Jacobé, the Maries of the town's name. Shunned by the Vatican, this paleo-Christian trio has a powerful hold on the Provençal psyche, with a captivating back story involving a boat journey from Palestine and a cameo from Mary Magdalene. Sara is the patron saint of the *gitans* (Roma people), and each 24 May, thousands come to town to pay their respects and party hard. Don't miss the ex-voto paintings that line the smoke-stained walls, personal petitions to Sara that are touching and startlingly strange in turns.

This town is the easiest spot to organise *promenades à cheval* (horseback riding); look for Fédération Française d'Equitation (FFE) accredited places, such as the friendly **Les Cabanes de Cacharel** (📞04 90 97 84 10; www.cabanesdecacharel. com) on the easterly D85A.

The Drive » The scenic D85A rejoins the D570, then, after 10 minutes or so, turn right into the D37. Stop at Méjanes for supplies or to visit the legendary fish restaurant Le Mazet du Caccarés. The D36B dramatically skims the eastern lakeshore; it's a 20-minute journey but is worth taking your time over.

- - - - - - - - - -

④ Étang de Vaccarès

This 600-sq-km lagoon, with its watery labyrinth of peninsulas and islands, is where the wetlands are at their most dense, almost primordial. Much of its tenuous shore forms the **Réserve Nationale**

de Camargue and is off-limits, making the wonderful nature trails and wildlife observatories at **La Capelière** (📞04 90 97 00 97; www.reserve-camargue. org; adult/child €3/1.50; ☺9am-1pm & 2-6pm Apr-Sep, 9am-1pm & 2-5pm Wed-Mon Oct-Mar; 🅿) particularly precious. The 1.5km-long **Sentier des Rainettes** (Tree-Frog Trail) takes you through tamarisk woodlands and the grasses of brackish open meadows.

The Drive » Continue on the D36B past Fiélouse for around 10 minutes.

- - - - - - - - - -

TRIP HIGHLIGHT

⑤ Salin de Badon

Before you leave **La Capelière**, grab your permits for another outstanding reserve site, once the **royal salt**

works (adult/child €3/1.50). Around the picturesque ruins are a number of observatories and 4.5km of wild trails – spy on flamingos wading through springtime iris. True birdwatchers mustn't miss a night in the **gîte** (dm €12) here, a bare-bones cottage in a priceless location.

The Drive » Continue south until you meet the D36, turning right. Stop in Salin de Giraud for bike hire and fuel (there's a 24/7 gas station) or visit the salt works. The D36 splits off to cross the Rhône via punt, but you continue south on the D36D, where it gets exciting: spectacular saltpans appear on your right, the river on your left.

- - - - - - - - - -

⑥ Domaine de la Palissade

Along the D36D, **Domaine de la Palissade** (📞04 42 86 81 28; www.palissade.fr; rte

---

DETOUR: AIGUES-MORTES

Start ③ Stes-Maries-de-la-Mer

Located over the border from Provence in the Gard, Aigues-Mortes sits a winding 28km northwest of Stes-Maries-de-la-Mer at the Camargue's far western extremity. Its central axis of streets often throngs with tourists, and shops spill out Camargue-themed tack, but the town is nonetheless magnificent, set in flat marshland and completely enclosed by rectangular ramparts and a series of towers. Come sundown, things change pace, and its squares are a lovely place to join locals for a relaxed *apéro* (predinner drink). Established by Louis IX in the mid-13th century to give the French crown a Mediterranean port, it was from here that the king launched the seventh Crusade (and persecuted Cathars). The **Tour de Constance** (adult/child €6.50/free; ☺10am-7pm May-Aug, 10am-5.30pm Sep-Apr) once held Huguenot prisoners; today it's the start of the 1.6km wall-top circuit, a must-do for heady views of salt mountains and viridian plains. Park on bd Diderot, on the outside of the northwestern wall.

Camargue horses

de la Mer; adult/child €3/free; ⊙9am-6pm mid-Jun–mid-Sep, to 5pm mid-Sep–mid-Nov & Mar–mid-Jun, to 5pm Wed-Sun mid-Nov–Feb) **organises horse treks** (from 1hr €8) where you'll find yourself wading across brackish lakes and through a purple haze of sea lavender. It will also take you around lagoons and scrubby glasswort on foot, or give you a free map of the estate's marked walking trails. Don't forget to rent binoculars;

best €2 you'll spend this trip!

The Drive » The next 3.7km along the rte de la Mer is equally enchanting, with flocks of birds circling and salt crystals flashing in the sun. Stop when you hit the sea.

- - - - - - - - - - -

TRIP HIGHLIGHT

❼ Plage de Piémanson

Just try and resist the urge to greet the Med with a wild dash into the waves at this lovely,

windswept beach. Unusually, camping is allowed here from May to September, and hundreds of campervans line up along the dunes for the duration of the *belle saison*. It's a scene that's as polarising of opinion as it is spectacular. Basic facilities and a patrolled section of sand are right at the end of rte de la Mer; head east for the popular nudist beach.

The Drive » Backtrack north along the D36D, just before

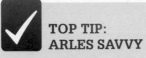

TOP TIP: ARLES SAVVY

Grab *Arles For Cool Tourists!*, a folding brochure with a simple city map and spot-on listings of restaurants, bars and shops. It also covers the Camargue.

Salin de Giraud, look for a car park and a small black shack on your right.

- - - - - - - - - - - - -

8 Le Point de Vue

This lookout provides a rare vantage point to take in the stunning scene of pink-stained *salins* (saltpans) and soaring crystalline mountains. As fruitful as it is beguiling, this is Europe's largest salt works, producing some 800,000 tonnes per year. A small shop (the aforementioned black shack) sells *sel de Camargue* (Camargue salt) by the pot or sack, bull sausages and tins of fragrant local olive oil.

The Drive » Heading north on D36 for 20 minutes, Le Mas de Peint is on your right before Le Sambuc, while La Chassagnette's fork and trowel shingle is on the left to its north.

- - - - - - - - - - - - -

9 Le Sambuc

This sleepy town's outskirts hide away a couple of the region's best restaurants and its most upscale lodgings. *Manadier* (bull estate owner) Jacques Bon, son of the family who owns hotel Le Mas de Peint, hosts Camargue farm-life demonstration days, **Journées Camarguaises** (📞04 90 97 28 50; www. manade-jacques-bon.com; adult/child incl lunch €38/19; 🕑monthly in summer), with music, *gardians* (cowboys) doing their thing and *taureau au feu de bois* (bull on the barbecue). But if it's boots-'n'-all *gardian* style you're after, pull up a stool at the roadside **Café du Sambuc** (rte du Sambuc): bull couscous and a jug of rosé for loose change, *and* staff adorned with

horse and Camargue cross tattoos.

The Drive » Continue north on the D36, where you'll re-meet the D570 heading to Arles, a 25km stretch in all.

- - - - - - - - - - - - -

🔟 Arles (p65)

Back in Arles, visit magnificent **Les Arènes** (Roman Amphithéâtre; adult/child incl Théâtre Antique €6.50/5; 🕑9am-7pm). Buy tickets for concerts at the **Bureau de Location** (box office; 📞08 91 70 03 70; www.arenes-arles.com; 🕑9.30am-noon & 2-6pm Mon-Fri, 10am-1pm Sat). Note, the Camargue take on the bullfight, the *course Camarguaise,* does not end in bloodshed. Well, not much. Rather, *razeteurs,* brave amateurs wearing skin-tight white shirts and trousers, snatch rosettes and ribbons tied to the horns of the *taureau* (bull) with a sharp comb. Victory is never as certain as the fact that, at some point, the bull will charge and the *razeteurs* will leap the arena's barrier, and the crowd will cheer.

Right: Les Arènes, Arles

Destinations

Nîmes & Around (p52)
A magnificient Roman amphitheatre, museums and markets compete for attention in this bustling commercial area.

Provence (p59)
With its picturesque lavender fields and delectable cuisine, Provence is a feast for the senses.

The French Riviera (p89)
Life's a beach in this idyllic region, as popular for its sun, sea and sand as it is for its arts scene.

Nîmes & Around

Nîmes is a busy commercial city these days, but two millennia ago it was one of the most important cities of Roman Gaul.

Links to Nîmes' past are clearly illustrated by the city's collection of Roman buildings, including a magnificent amphitheatre and 2000-year-old temple.

There are plenty of museums and markets to explore, as well as a host of high-profile festivals throughout the year. Nîmes is also famous for its contribution to global couture – namely the hard-wearing twill fabric known as *serge de Nîmes,* traditionally worn by agricultural labourers, and nowadays known to all as denim.

◉ Sights

★ Les Arènes   Roman Sites

(www.arenes-nimes.com; place des Arènes; adult/child €9/7; ⊙9am-8pm Jul & Aug, shorter hours rest of year) Nîmes' twin-tiered amphitheatre is the best-preserved in France. Built around 100 BC, the arena would have seated 24,000 spectators and staged gladiatorial contests and public executions, and it still provides an impressive venue for gigs, events and summer bullfights. An audioguide provides context as you explore the arena, seating areas, stairwells and corridors (rather marvellously known to Romans as *vomitories*), and afterwards you can view replicas of gladiatorial armour and original bullfighters' costumes in the museum.

At 133m long, 101m wide and 21m high, with an oval arena encircled by two tiers

of arches and columns, the amphitheatre is a testament to the skill and ingenuity of Roman architects. Despite being adapted, plundered for stone and generally abused over many centuries, the structure of the amphitheatre is still largely intact, and it's not hard to imagine what the atmosphere must have been like when it was filled to capacity.

The seating is divided into four tiers and 34 rows; the posher you were, the closer you sat to the centre. The amphitheatre's oval design meant everyone had an unrestricted view. A system of trap-doors and hoist-lifts beneath the arena enabled animals and combatants to be put into position during the show. Originally, the amphitheatre would have had a canopy that protected spectators from the weather.

Since 2012 a project has been underway to clean limescale and pollution stains from the exterior, so there may be scaffolding when you visit.

Maison Carrée   Roman Sites

(place de la Maison Carrée; adult/child €5.50/4; ⊙10am-8pm Jul & Aug, shorter hours rest of year) Constructed in gleaming limestone around AD 5, this temple was built to honour Emperor Augustus' two adopted sons. Despite the name, the Maison Carrée (Square House) is actually rectangular – to the Romans, 'square' simply meant a building with right angles. The building is beautifully

Jardins de la Fontaine

preserved, complete with stately columns and triumphal steps; it's worth paying the admission to see the interior, but probably worth skipping the lame 3D film.

Jardins de la Fontaine — Roman Sites

(Tour Magne adult/child €3.20/2.70; ⊘ Tour Magne 9.30am-6.30pm) The elegant Jardins de la Fontaine conceal several Roman remains, most notably the 30m-high **Tour Magne**, raised around 15 BC. Built as a display of imperial power, it's the largest of a chain of towers that at once punctuated the city's 7km-long Roman ramparts. At the top of its 140 steps, there's an orientation table to help you interpret the panorama over Nîmes.

Elsewhere around the gardens are the **Source de la Fontaine** – once the site of a spring, temple and baths – and the crumbling **Temple de Diane**, located in the gardens' northwest corner.

Carré d'Art — Museum

(www.carreartmusee.com; place de la Maison Carrée; permanent collection free, exhibitions adult/child €5 /3.70; ⊘10am-6pm Tue-Sun) The striking glass-and-steel building facing the Maison Carrée was designed by British architect Sir Norman Foster. Inside is the **municipal library** and the **Musée d'Art Contemporain**, with permanent and temporary exhibitions covering art from the 1960s onwards. The rooftop restaurant makes a lovely spot for lunch.

Musée du Vieux Nîmes — Museum

(place aux Herbes; ⊘10am-6pm Tue-Sun) **FREE** The town museum delves into the history of Nîmes from Roman times through to the modern era, with lots of period costumes and a display of denim-wearing celebrities including Elvis and Marilyn Monroe. Located inside Nîmes' 17th-century episcopal palace.

Musée Archéologique — Archaeological Museum

(13 bd Amiral Courbet; ⊘10am-6pm Tue-Sun) **FREE** Nîmes' archaeological museum has a collection of Roman tombs, mosaics and other artifacts unearthed around the city. There's an intriguing display on the city's Iron Age origins and its massive transformation during the Roman era.

ℹ INFO: PASS NÎMES ROMAINE

A joint ticket (adult/child €11.50/9) covers admission to Les Arènes, Maison Carrée and Tour Magne, and remains valid for three days.

All three sites have the same closing hours: 8pm in July and August; 7pm in June; 6.30pm in April, May and September; 6pm in March and October; and 5.30pm from November to February.

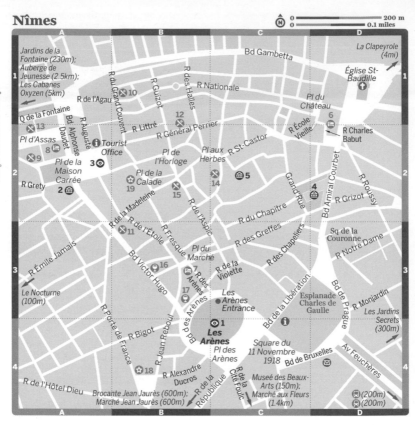

Musée d'Histoire Naturelle   Museum

(13 bd Amiral Courbet; ☺10am-6pm Tue-Sun) **FREE**
Sharing the same building as the Musée Arch éologique, the Natural History Museum ha s the usual displays of stuffed beasties, fossils and skeletons, as well as a few men- hi rs decorated by prehistoric artists. Don't forget to say *bonjour* to Maurice the stuffed giraffe as you enter.

Musée des Beaux-Arts   Art Museum

(rue de la Cité Foulc; ☺10am-6pm Tue-Sun) **FREE**
Th e city's fine-arts museum has a fairly pe destrian collection of Flemish, Italian an d French works, although it's worth a look for the fine Roman mosaic that can be viewed from the 1st floor. Entry to the perma nent collection is free. Located about 200m south of Les Arènes.

🎎 Festivals & Events

Les Grands Jeux Romains   Event

Fo r two days in mid-April, Romans again take over town with an encampment, staged gl adiatorial battles in Les Arènes and a tri- umphal street parade.

Féria de Pentecôte & Féria des Vendanges   Bullfighting

Nî mes becomes more Catalan than French during its two *férias* (bullfighting festivals): the five-day Féria de Pentecôte (Whitsuntide Festival) in June, and the three-day Féria des Vendanges on the third weekend in September. Each is marked by daily bullfights.

Jeudis de Nîmes   Festival

Between 6pm and 10.30pm every Thursday in July and August, food markets and live gigs take over Nîmes' squares.

Nîmes

◎ Top Sights

◎ Sights

◎ Sleeping

◎ Eating

◎ Drinking & Nightlife

◎ Entertainment

◎ Sleeping

Auberge de Jeunesse Hostel €
(☑04 66 68 03 20; www.hinimes.com; 257 chemin de l'Auberge de Jeunesse, La Cigale; dm/d €16.45/38; ☉reception 7.30am-1am) It's out in the sticks, 4km from the bus and train stations, but this hostel has lots in its favour: spacious dorms, family rooms, a garden with space for camping, and a choice of self-catering kitchen or cafe. Take bus 1, direction Alès or Villeverte, and get off at the Stade stop.

Hôtel Central Hotel €
(☑04 66 67 27 75; www.hotel-central.org; 2 place du Château; d €60-95, f €90-125) If you like your lines clean and your clutter minimal, this recently modernised hotel will suit you nicely. The rooms have been renovated with wooden floors, neutral colours and sleek bathrooms, with exposed stone left for character;

superieur rooms offer the most space. The lack of lift is a drawback considering the number of stairs. Ring ahead to ask staff to reserve you a parking space.

★ Hôtel de l'Amphithéâtre Hotel €€
(☑04 66 67 28 51; www.hoteldelamphitheatre.com; 4 rue des Arènes; s/d/f €72/92/130) Down a narrow backstreet leading away from Les Arènes, this tall townhouse ticks all the boxes: smart rooms with shabby-chic furniture and balconies overlooking the place du Marché; a sleek palette of greys, whites and taupes; and a great buffet breakfast. It's run by an expat Cornishman and his French wife.

Les Cabanes Oxyzen Cottages €€
(☑04 66 84 99 80; www.chambres-hotes-nimes.com; 80 impasse du Couchant; d €140-150; 🐾🏊) Fabulous fun: three ultra-contemporary timber cabins, arranged around a lush Mediterranean garden and swimming pool shaded by oaks and strawberry trees. Each cabin has its own letter theme (X for XXL, Y for Yellow, Z for Zen) with corresponding decor. It's 6km northwest of the centre.

Royal Hôtel Hotel €€
(☑04 66 58 28 27; www.royalhotel-nimes.com; 3 bd Alphonse Daudet; d €82-102, f €163; 🏊🐾) This upmarket hotel offers grace and style. Bedrooms have a choice of street views or an outlook over the grand place d'Assas. They're split into standard and superior, all with modern-meets-heritage decor; it's worth bumping up a level for extra space and air-con. The downstairs restaurant, La Bodeguita, offers solid Med dining.

La Clapeyrole B&B, Self-Contained €€
(☑04 66 26 85 06; 222 impasse de la Clapeyrole; d per night €120-130, per week €700-900; 🏊) This detached house is a stunner, set among the wooded hills above Nîmes, about 10 minutes' drive from the centre. Modern lines, minimalist decor and a pool encircled by olive trees provide a level of indulgence that normally costs twice the price. It's about 7km northeast of town, off the D979.

Les Jardins Secrets B&B €€€
(☑04 66 84 82 64; www.jardinssecrets.net; 3 rue Gaston Maruejols; d €195-380, ste €380-450; 🐾) For doing Nîmes en luxe, nowhere tops the Secret Gardens. Decorated to resemble an 18th-century *maison bourgeoise* (townhouse), it's dripping with luxury, from

chaise longues and antique clawfoot baths to a wonderful Roman-style bathhouse and divine gardens – but for these kind of prices, you'd think they could include breakfast and parking (an extra €25 and €20 respectively).

Hôtel Imperator Concorde — Hotel €€€
(☎04 66 21 90 30; www.nimes.concorde-hotels.com; quai de la Fontaine; r from €180) Nîmes' longstanding grand hotel, with a guest list that's taken in everyone from famous matadors to European aristocrats (and Hemingway, of course). It's staid in style, heavy on drapes and heritage furniture, but some of the rooms are looking seriously dated.

✕ Eating

Nîmes' gastronomy owes as much to the spicy flavours of Provence as to the meaty richness of the Languedoc.

La Petite Fadette — Cafe €
(☎04 66 67 53 05; 34 rue du Grand Couvent; menus €9.50-14.50; ⊘8am-7pm) Salads and crispy *tartines* (open toasted sandwiches) are the order of the day at this homely cafe, with a cute rococo interior lined with vintage photos, and outside tables on a small courtyard on the rue du Grand Couvent. The food isn't fancy, but portions are huge: try the smoked salmon or the cured ham and goat's cheese.

★ Le Cerf à Moustache — Bistro €€
(☎09 81 83 44 33; 38 bd Victor Hugo; mains €14-35; ⊘11.45am-2pm & 7-11pm Tue-Sat) Despite its weird name, the Deer with the Moustache has quickly established itself as one of Nîmes' top bistros, with quirky decor (including reclaimed furniture and a wall full of old-book doodles), matched by chef Julien Salem's creative take on the classics. Go basic with burgers and risotto, or upmarket with crusted lamb and chunky steaks.

L'Imprévu — Modern French €€
(☎04 66 38 99 59; www.l-imprevu.com; 6 place d'Assas; mains €19.50-27.50; ⊘noon-2pm & 7-10pm Thu-Mon) A fine-dining French bistro tucked in the corner of place d'Assas, with an open-plan kitchen and a cute interior courtyard. There's a good choice of seafood and meats, from sea bass in balsamic vinaigrette to thyme-marinated lamb. Dishes are mainly à la carte, although there's a limited *menu du jour* (set menu).

Le Nocturne — Bistro €€
(☎04 66 67 20 28; www.restaurant-le-nocturne.com; 29bis rue Benoît Malon; mains €20-30; ⊘8pm-2am) Swish but not snooty, this is a fine place to dine on rich southwest flavours. Duck, foie gras and mushrooms feature heavily – in fact, you can have your duck breast with a choice of four sauces (raspberry, apple, cep or morel), try a classic *confit de canard* (duck cooked in its own fat) or even try it *au tartare* (served raw). It's on rue Benoît Malon, about 10 minutes' walk west of Les Arènes.

Carré d'Art — Gastronomic €€
(☎04 66 67 52 40; www.restaurant-lecarredart.fr; 2 rue Gaston Boissier; lunch/dinner menu €19.50/32; ⊘noon-3pm & 7.30-10pm Tue-Sat) Open since 1989, this gastronomic heavy-hitter is still one of Nîmes' top fine-dining addresses. The setting is elegant, in a 19th-century townhouse decked out with abstract art and a gorgeous shaded courtyard, and the food gives traditional French a modern spin: mackerel escabèche, or Provençal sea bass with aubergine caviar.

Self-Catering

Les Halles — Market
(rue Guizot, rue Général Perrier & rue des Halles; ⊘6.30am-1pm) Nîmes' covered market is the best place for supplies: look out for local specialities including *picholines* (a local green olive with its own AOC) and *brandade* (salt cod).

Maison Villaret — Boulangerie
(13 rue de la Madeleine; ⊘8am-6pm Mon-Sat, to 1pm Sun) This family *boulangerie* (bakery) makes 25 different kinds of bread, cakes and biscuits, such as *caladons* (honey and almond-studded biscuits).

L'Oustaù Nadal — Delicatessen
(place aux Herbes; ⊘9am-5pm Tue-Sat) Goodies such as tapenade, honey and olive oil (including three kinds on tap).

🍷 Drinking & Nightlife

Place aux Herbes, place de l'Horloge and place du Marché are packed with busy cafes.

Grand Café de la Bourse et du Commerce — Bar
(bd des Arènes; ⊘8am-midnight) Step back in time to a more elegant era at this opulent

19 th-century cafe opposite Les Arènes, gleaming with chandeliers and mirrors.

Café Olive Bar

(☑04 66 67 89 10; 22 bd Victor Hugo; ⊙9am-1pm Mon-Sat) A lively little nightspot, the stone wa lls and dim lighting of which give it a cosy cavern vibe. There are regular gigs and a great choice of wines by the glass.

☆ Entertainment

Les Arènes is the major venue for outdoor sp ectacles such as concerts, pageants and bullfights.

Ciné Sémaphore Cinema

(☑04 66 67 83 11; www.cinema-semaphore.fr; 25 rue Porte de France) Five screens showing *version originale* (VO, or nondubbed) films.

Théâtre de Nîmes Performing Arts

(☑04 66 36 02 04; www.theatredenimes.com; place de la Calade) Renowned venue for drama and music.

🛍 Shopping

Regular markets are held in Nîmes through-out the week.

Brocante Jean Jaurès Flea Market

(Flea Market; bd Jean Jaurès; ⊙8am-1pm Mon)

Marché Jean Jaurès Farmers Market

(F armers Market; bd Jean Jaurès; ⊙7am-1pm Fri) Held at the same place as the flea market.

Marché aux Fleurs Flower Market

(F lower Market; ⊙7am-6pm Mon) Held outside the Stade des Costières.

ℹ Information

Tourist Office (☑04 66 58 38 00; www.ot -nimes.fr; 6 rue Auguste; ⊙8.30am-8pm Mon-Fri, 9am-7pm Sat, 10am-6pm Sun Jul & Aug, shorter hours rest of year) There's also a seasonal an-nexe (usually open July and August) on esplanade Charles de Gaulle.

ℹ Getting There & Away

AIR

Nîmes' **airport** (☑04 66 70 49 49; www.nimes-aeroport.fr), 10km southeast of the city on the A54, is served only by Ryanair, which flies to/from London Luton, Liverpool, Brussels and Fez.

An airport bus (€5.50, 30 minutes) connects with all flights to/from the train station.

CAR & MOTORCYCLE

Major car-rental companies have kiosks at the airport and the train station.

AROUND NÎMES

◉ Sights & Activities

★ Pont du Gard Roman Sites

(☑04 66 37 50 99; www.pontdugard.fr; car & up to 5 passengers €18, after 8pm €10; ⊙visitor centre & mu seum 9am-8pm Jul & Aug, shorter hours rest of year) Southern France has some fine Roman sites, but nothing can top the Unesco World He ritage Site–listed Pont du Gard, 21km no rtheast of Nîmes. This fabulous three-ti ered aqueduct was once part of a 50km-long system of water channels, built around 19 BC to transport water from Uzès to Nîmes. Th e scale is huge: 48.8m high, 275m long an d graced with 35 precision-built arches; the bridge was sturdy enough to carry up to 20,000 cubic metres of water per day.

Each block was carved by hand and trans-ported from nearby quarries – no mean feat, considering the largest blocks weight over 5 to nnes. Amazingly, the height of the bridge descends by just 2.5cm across its length, pro-viding just enough gradient to keep the water flowing – an amazing demonstration of the precision of Roman engineering. The Musée de la Romanité provides background on the bridge's construction, and the Ludo play area helps kids to learn in a fun, hands-on way.

You can walk across the tiers for panoram-ic views over the Gard River, but the best per-spective on the bridge is from downstream, along the 1.4km Mémoires de Garrigue walk-ing trail. Early evening is a good time to visit, as admission is cheaper and the bridge is stunningly illuminated after dark.

There are large car parks on both banks of the river, 400m walk from the bridge. Several buses stop nearby, including Edgard bus B21 (hourly Monday to Saturday, two or three on Sunday) from Nîmes to Alès.

Perrier Plant Water Factory

(☑04 66 87 61 01; www.visitez-perrier.com/en; ad ult/child €3/1, tours €4/2; ⊙10am-4pm Mon-Fri) Nîmes isn't only famous for denim – it's also the home of Perrier, the world-famous fizzy water, which has its source in natural springs 13km southwest of the city. The main plant supplies around 900 million bottles of water

✓ TOP TIP: CANOEING ON THE GARD RIVER

For a unique perspective on the Pont du Gard, you need to see it from the water. The Gard River flows down from the Cévennes mountains all the way to the aqueduct, passing through the dramatic Gorges du Gardon en route. The best time to do it is in spring between April and June, as winter floods and summer droughts can sometimes make the river impassable.

Most of the local hire companies are based in Collias, 8km from the bridge, a journey of about two hours by kayak. Depending on the season and the height of the river, you can make a longer journey by being dropped upstream at Pont St Nicholas (19km, four to five hours) or Russan (32km, six to seven hours); the latter option also includes a memorable trip through the Gorges du Gardon.

Most companies are open from around 8am to 6pm in summer. There's a minimum age of six, and life-jackets are always provided.

Canoë Collias (☑04 66 22 87 20; www.canoe-collias.com; from Collias adult/child €22/12, from Russan €35/16)

Kayak Vert (☑04 66 22 80 76; www.kayakvert.com; from Collias adult/child €22/11, from Russan €41/20)

Le Tourbillon (☑04 66 22 85 54; www.canoe-le-tourbillon.com; from Collias adult/child €22/11, from Russan €35/22)

every year; you can visit the factory and watch a 3D film that explains Perrier's history, the production process, and the reason behind the bottle's iconic shape (spoiler: it's to do with pressure). Remember to pick up Perrier-themed souvenirs in the shop.

Guided tours visit the bottling plant itself, but are only in French.

Uzès

POP 8450

Twenty-five kilometres northeast of Nîmes, the trim little town of Uzès is renowned for its graceful Renaissance architecture, a reminder of the days when this was an important trading centre – especially for silk, linen and, bizarrely, liquorice.

The key sights are the ducal palace and the arcaded central square, place aux Herbes, which hosts a lively farmers market every Wednesday and Saturday.

👁 Sights & Activities

Duché   Château

(www.duche-uzes.fr; admission €13, incl guided tour adult/child €18/7; ⊙10am-12.30pm & 2-6.30pm) This fortified château belonged to the House of Cressol, who were the Dukes of Uzès for more than 1000 years until the Revolution.

The building is a Renaissance wonder, with a majestic 16th-century façade showing the three orders of classical architecture (Ionic, Doric and Corinthian). Inside, you can take a guided tour (in French) of the lavish ducal apartments and 800-year-old cellars, and climb the Bermonde tower for town views.

Jardin Médiéval   Garden

(Medieval Garden; adult/child €4.50/2; ⊙10.30am-12.30pm & 2-6pm Apr-Oct) This delightful garden contains a wealth of plants and flowers that served various purposes for their medieval planters: medicinal, nutritional and symbolic.

Musée du Bonbon Haribo   Museum

(Candy Museum; www.museeharibo.fr; Pont des Charrettes; adult/child €7/4.50; ⊙10am-1pm & 2-6pm Tue-Sun Oct-Jun, daily Jul-Sep) Uzès' history as a centre for confectionery continues at this Wonka-esque museum, which explores the sweet-making process from the early 20th century through to the present day. There's a collection of antique advertising posters and vintage confectionery machinery, but inevitably it's the rainbow-coloured sweet shop that takes centre stage.

ⓘ Information

Tourist Office (☑04 66 22 68 88; www.uzes-tourisme.com; place Albert 1er; ⊙10am-6pm Mon-Fri, 10am-1pm & 2-5pm Sat & Sun)

Provence

Provence evokes picture-postcard images of lavender fields, medieval hilltop villages, bustling markets and superb food and wine.

While the Vaucluse and Luberon epitomise the Provençal cliché, if you go a little deeper, you'll find Provence's incredible diversity. Near the mouth of the Rhône in the Camargue, craggy limestone yields to bleached salt marshes specked pink with flamingos, and the light, which so captivated Van Gogh and Cézanne, begins to change. Then there's the serpentine Gorges du Verdon, its pea-green water lorded over by half-mile-high limestone walls and craggy mountain peaks beyond. The region's other *belle surprises* are its cities: bohemian Aix and Roman Arles.

Constant across the region is the food – clean, bright flavours, as simple as sweet tomatoes drizzled with olive oil and sprinkled with *fleur de sel* (sea salt) from the Camargue.

History

Settled over the centuries by the Ligurians, the Celts and the Greeks, the area between the Alps, the sea and the Rhône River flourished following Julius Caesar's conquest in the mid-1st century BC. The Romans called the area Provincia Romana, which evolved into the name Provence. After the collapse of the Roman Empire in the late 5th century Provence was invaded several times, by the Visigoths, Burgundians and Ostrogoths.

During the 14th century, the Catholic Church, under a series of French-born popes, moved its headquarters from feud-riven Rome to Avignon, thus beginning the most resplendent period in the city's (and region's) history. Provence became part of France in 1481, but Avignon and Carpentras remained under papal control until the Revolution.

Aix-en-Provence

POP 144,274

Aix-en-Provence, 25km from Marseille, is to Provence what the Left Bank is to Paris: an enclave of bourgeois-bohemian chic. Some 30,000 students from the Université de Provence Aix-Marseille, many from overseas, set the mood on the street: bars, cafes and affordable restaurants. The city is rich in culture (two of Aix' most famous sons are Paul Cézanne and Émile Zola) and oh-so respectable, with plane-tree-shaded boulevards and fashionable boutiques. All this class comes at a price: Aix is more expensive than other Provençal towns.

⊙ Sights & Activities

A stroller's paradise, the highlight is the mostly pedestrian old city, Vieil Aix. South of cours Mirabeau, the Quartier Mazarin was laid out in the 17th century, and is home to some of Aix' finest buildings and a square: place des Quatre Dauphins, with its fish-spouting fountain (1667), is enchanting.

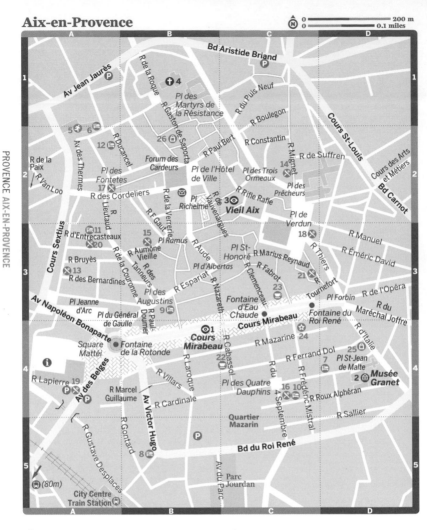

★ **Cours Mirabeau**   Historic Quarter

No avenue better epitomises Provence's most graceful city than this fountain-studded street, sprinkled with Renaissance *hôtels particuliers* (private mansions) and crowned with a summertime roof of leafy plane trees. Named after the revolutionary hero Comte de Mirabeau, it was laid out in the 1640s. Cézanne and Zola hung out at **Les Deux Garçons** (53 cours Mirabeau; ⊙7am-2am), one of a clutch of busy pavement cafes.

★ **Musée Granet**   Museum

(www.museegranet-aixenprovence.fr; place St-Jean de Malte; adult/child €7/free; ⊙11am-7pm Tue-Sun) Housed in a 17th-century priory of the Knights of Malta, this exceptional museum is named after the Provençal painter François Marius Granet (1775–1849), who donated a large number of works. Its collection includes 16th- to 20th-century Italian, Flemish and French works. Modern art reads like a who's who: Picasso, Léger, Matisse, Monet, Klee, Van Gogh and Giacometti, among others, including the museum's

Aix-en-Provence

pride and joy: nine Cézanne works. Excellent temporary exhibitions.

Cathédrale St-Sauveur Church

(rue de la Roque; ⊙8am-noon & 2-6pm) Built between 1285 and 1350 in a potpourri of styles, this cathedral includes a Romanesque 12th-century nave in its southern aisle, chapels from the 14th and 15th centuries, and a 5th-century sarcophagus in the apse. More recent additions include the 18th-century gilt baroque organ. Acoustics make Sunday-afternoon Gregorian chants unforgettable.

Fondation Victor Vasarely Gallery

(☎04 42 20 01 09; www.fondationvasarely.fr; 1 av Marcel Pagnol; adult/child €9/4; ⊙10am-1pm & 2-6pm Tue-Sun; ⬜4 or 6 stop Vasarely) This gallery, 4km west of the city, was designed by Hungarian optical-art innovator Victor Vasarely (1906-97). A masterpiece, its 16 interconnecting six-walled galleries were purpose-built to display and reflect the patterning of the artist's 44 acid-trip-ready, floor-to-ceiling geometric artworks.

Thermes Sextius Spa

(☎04 42 23 81 82; www.thermes-sextius.com; 55 av des Thermes; day pass from €99) These modern thermal spas are built on the site of Roman Aquae Sextiae's springs, whose excavated remains are displayed beneath glass in the lobby.

✯ Festivals & Events

Festival d'Aix-en-Provence Performing Arts

(☎04 34 08 02 17; www.festival aix.com; ⊙Jul) Month-long festival of classical music, opera, ballet and buskers.

◯ Sleeping

Hôtel les Quatre Dauphins Boutique Hotel €

(☎04 42 38 16 39; www.lesquatredauphins.fr; 54 rue Roux Alphéran; s €62-72, d €72-87; ❄⊛) This sweet 13-room hotel slumbers in a former private mansion in one of the loveliest parts of town. Rooms are fresh and clean, with excellent modern bathrooms. Those with sloping, beamed ceilings in the attic are quaint but not for those who cannot pack light – the terracotta-tiled staircase is not suitcase-friendly.

Hôtel Cardinal Hotel €

(☎04 42 38 32 30; www.hotel-cardinal-aix.com; 24 rue Cardinale; s/d €68/78; ⊛) Slightly rumpled rooms are quaintly furnished with antiques and tasselled curtains. There are also six gigantic suites in the annexe up the street, each with a kitchenette and dining room, which are ideal for longer stays.

★ DON'T MISS:
CÉZANNE SIGHTS

The life of local lad Paul Cézanne (1839–1906) is treasured in Aix. To see where he ate, drank, studied and painted, follow the Circuit de Cézanne (Cézanne Trail), marked by footpath-embedded bronze plaques. Pick up the accompanying information booklet at the tourist office.

Cézanne's last studio, Atelier Cézanne (www.atelier-cezanne.com; 9 av Paul Cézanne; adult/child €5.50/€2; ⊘10am-noon & 2-5pm), 1.5km north of the tourist office on a hilltop, was painstakingly preserved (and recreated: not all the tools and still-life models strewn around the single room were his) as it was at the time of his death. Though the studio is inspiring, none of his works hang here. Films are screened in the garden in July and August. Further uphill is the Terrain des Peintres, a terraced garden perfect for a picnic, from where Cézanne painted the Montagne Ste-Victoire.

Visits to the other two sights must be reserved in advance at the tourist office. In 1859 Cézanne's father bought Le Jas de Bouffan (☑04 42 16 10 91; adult/child €5.50/2; ⊘guided tours 10.30am-5.30pm; ☐6 stop Corsy), a country manor west of Aix' centre, where Cézanne painted furiously: 36 oils and 17 watercolours in the decades that followed depicting the house, farm and chestnut-lined alley. It's a 20-minute walk from town.

In 1895 Cézanne rented a cabin at Les Carrières de Bibémus (Bibémus Quarries; ☑04 42 16 10 91; 3090 chemin de Bibémus; adult/child €5.50/2; ⊘guided tour 9.45am Jun-Sep, less frequently rest of year), on the edge of town, where he painted prolifically and where he did most of his Montagne Ste-Victoire paintings. Atmospheric one-hour tours of the ochre quarry take visitors on foot through the dramatic burnt-orange rocks Cézanne captured so vividly.

★ L'Épicerie
B&B €€

(☑06 08 85 38 68; www.unechambreenville.eu; 12 rue du Cancel; d €100-130; 🖥🏠) This intimate B&B is the fabulous creation of born-and-bred Aixois lad Luc. His breakfast room re-creates a 1950s grocery store, and the flowery garden out back is perfect for excellent evening dining and weekend brunch (book ahead for both). Breakfast is a veritable feast. Two rooms accommodate families of four.

Hôtel des Augustins
Hotel €€

(☑04 42 27 28 59; www.hotel-augustins.com; 3 rue de la Masse; d €109-249; ✳🏠) A heartbeat from the hub of Aixois life, this former 15th-century convent with magnificent stone-vaulted lobby and sweeping staircase has volumes of history: Martin Luther stayed here after his excommunication from Rome. Filled with hand-painted furniture, the largest, most luxurious rooms have jacuzzis; two rooms have private terraces beneath the filigreed bell tower.

Le Manoir
Hotel €€

(☑04 42 26 27 20; www.hotelmanoir.com; 8 rue d'Entrecasteux; d €82-126, tr €114; ⊘Feb-Dec; 🖥🏠) Atmospherically set in a 14th-century cloister, the Manor – an easy family choice –

is something of a blast from the past. Old world in spirit and location, it sits in an uncannily quiet wedge of the old town. Rooms are clean, simple and bourgeois spacious. Best up is the free parking in the gravel courtyard out front and breakfast, served alfresco in a vaulted cloister.

Hôtel Aquabella
Spa Hotel €€€

(☑04 42 99 15 00; www.aquabella.fr; 3 rue des Étuves; d/tr €210/230) Should wallowing like a Roman in Aix-en-Provence's thermal waters tickle your fancy, then check into this three-star hotel adjoining the Thermes Sextius spa. Rates include spa access and there is really nothing more delightful after a hard day boutique shopping than a lounge in the eucalypt-scented hammam followed by a dip in the outdoor pool, with a view of Roman ruins.

Hôtel Cézanne
Boutique Hotel €€€

(☑04 42 91 11 11; http://cezanne.hotelaix.com; 40 av Victor Hugo; s/d €230/260; ✳@🏠) Purple flags fly proud outside Aix' swishest hotel, a contemporary study in clean lines, with sharp-edged built-in desks, top-end fabrics and design-driven decor. In any other city its location next to the train station would be deemed a flaw. Reserve ahead for free parking.

Cathédrale St-Sauveur (p61), Aix-en-Provence

INFO: AIX-CELLENT

The Aix City Pass (€15), valid for five days, includes a guided walking tour, admission to the Atelier Cézanne, Jas de Bouffan and Musée Granet, and a trip on the minitram; the Cézanne Pass (€12) covers his three main sights. Buy passes at the tourist office or at any of the sights.

✕ Eating

Aix excels at Provençal cuisine and restaurant terraces spill out across dozens and dozens of charm-heavy old town squares, many pierced with an ancient stone fountain: place des Trois Ormeaux, place des Augustins, place Ramus and vast Forum des Cadeurs are particular favourites.

★ Jacquou
Le Croquant   Southwest, Provençal €

(☑ 04 42 27 37 19; www.jacquoulecroquant.com; 2 rue de l'Aumône Vielle; plat du jour €10.90, menus from €14; ⊗ noon-3pm & 7-11pm) This veteran address, around since 1985, stands out on dozens of counts: buzzy jovial atmosphere, flowery patio garden, funky interior, early evening opening, family friendly, hearty homecooking, a *menu* covering all price ranges, and so forth. Cuisine from southwestern France is its speciality, meaning lots of duck, but the vast menu covers all bases.

La Tarte Tropézienne   Patisserie, Cafe €

(av des Belges; sandwich/salad menu €6.90/7.35, mains €12-14) A handy stop en route to/from the bus and train stations, this modern patisserie is known for its sugar-encrusted *tarte Tropézienne* (cream-filled sandwich cake from St-Tropez), displayed in cabinets like jewels beneath glass. Grab a wedge (€2.90) to take out or eat in – on red director chairs on a decking terrace. Excellent-value gourmet sandwiches and salads.

Charlotte   Bistro €

(☑ 04 42 26 77 56; 32 rue des Bernardines; 2-/3-course menus €16.50/20; ⊗ 12.30-2pm & 8-10.30pm Tue-Sat; 🖼) It's all very cosy at Charlotte, where everyone knows everyone. French classics such as veal escalope and beef steak are mainstays, and there is always a vegetarian dish and a couple of imaginative *plats du jour* (dishes of the day). In summer everything moves into the garden.

La Bidule   Bistro €

(☑ 04 42 26 87 75; www.brasserielebidule.fr; 8 rue Lieutaud; mains €12.50-15; ⊗ 9am-11.30pm) Of the many restaurant terraces on elongated square Forum des Cadeurs, 'The Thingy' is hot with students and late-lunch diners. Its sizable terrace with colourful flowery tablecloths and fairy lights at night is made for lingering, and the fare is hearty bistro – the honey-roasted camembert, burgers and fiesty salads are all superb. Excellent-value lunch *menus* include a glass of wine or coffee.

Le Petit Verdot   French €€

(☑ 04 42 27 30 12; www.lepetitverdot.fr; 7 rue d'Entrecasteaux; mains €15-25; ⊗ 7pm-midnight Mon-Sat) Delicious *menus* are designed around what's in season, and paired with excellent wines. Meats are often braised all day, vegetables are tender, stewed in delicious broths. Save room for an incandescent dessert. Lively dining occurs around tabletops made of wine crates (expect to talk to your neighbour), and the gregarious owner speaks multiple languages.

Jardin Mazarin   French €€

(☑ 04 42 58 11 42; www.jardinmazarin.com; 15 rue du 4 Sepembre; menu €34, mains €15-20; ⊗ noon-2.30pm & 8-10.30pm Tue-Sat) Something of a hidden address, this elegant restaurant serenades the ravishing *hôtel particulier* in which it languishes. Two salons sit beneath splendid beamed ceilings, but the real gem is outside: a luxurious green garden with fountain and a line-up of tables beneath a wicker shade. Peace, perfect peace, far from the madding crowd.

Petit Pierre Reboul   Gastronomic €€€

(☑ 04 42 52 30 42; www.restaurant-pierre-reboul.com; 11 Petite Rue St-Jean; 2-/3-course bistro menu €19-34/27-39, gastronomic menus €52 & €87; ⊗ noon-2.30pm & 7.30-10.30pm Tue-Sat) This brightly coloured address, hidden down a back alley, is the bistro arm of Pierre Reboul's gastronomic restaurant next door. The vibe is contemporary design (think acid-bright fabrics and lampshades made from pencils), and the *menu* throws in the odd adventurous dish alongside mainstream stalwarts such as burgers, Caesar salad, grilled meats and mussels'n'fries.

🍷 Drinking & Nightlife

The scene is fun, but fickle. For nightlife, hit rue de la Verrerie and place Richelme. Open-air cafes crowd the city's squares, especially Forum des Cardeurs, place de Verdun and place de l'Hôtel de Ville, and the city has a clutch of cinemas.

Book in Bar   Cafe

(4 rue Cabassol; ⊙ 9am-7pm Mon-Sat) There is no more literary spot to partake in *un café* than this particularly fine English bookshop with cafe. Look out for occasional book readings, jazz evenings et al.

La Mado   Cafe

(Chez Madeleine; ☑ 04 42 38 28 02; www.lamado -aix.com; 4 place des Prêcheurs; lunch/dinner menus €18/32; ⊙ 7am-2am) This smart daytime cafe, with steel-grey parasols and boxed-hedge terrace on a busy square, is unbeatable for coffee and fashionable-people watching; its food, lunch or dinner, is equally excellent. The Mado has been around for years, so the old guard dine while the hipsters shine.

Le Mistral   Club

(www.mistralclub.fr; 3 rue Frédéric Mistral; ⊙ 11.30pm-6am Tue-Sat) If anyone's awake past midnight, chances are they'll wind up at this happening basement club, with three bars and a dance floor. DJs spin house, R&B, techno and rap.

🛍 Shopping

Chic fashion boutiques cluster along pedestrian rue Marius Reynaud and cours Mirabeau. But it is at the daily morning market on place Richelme, piled high with marinated olives, goat-milk cheese, lavender, honey, fruit and a bounty of other seasonal foods, that you'll find the local Aixois crowd. Or try the Sunday-morning flower market on place des Prêcheurs.

Farinoman Fou   Boulangerie

(3 rue Mignet; ⊙ Tue-Sat) Tucked just off place des Prêcheurs is this truly phenomenal bakery, which has a constant queue outside its door. The crunchy, different-flavoured breads baked by artisan boulanger Benoît Fradette are reason enough to sell up and move to Aix. The bakery has no shop as such; customers jostle for space with bread ovens and dough-mixing tubs.

La Chambre aux Confitures   Preserves

(www.lachambreauxconfitures.com; 16bis rue d'Italie; ⊙ 10am-1pm & 3-7pm Mon-Fri, 10am-7.30pm Sat, 10am-1pm Sun) Do as locals do: don't be shy about asking to taste a jam, chutney or jelly in this outstanding boutique bursting with exotic and unexpected flavours. Best-selling jams include clementine and *calisson* (marzipan-like chewy delicacy), apricot and lavender, and nutty fig and cognac. Excellent chutneys too, for pairing with cheese, meat and foie gras.

ℹ Information

Tourist Office (☑ 04 42 16 11 61; www.aixen provencetourism.com; square Colonel Antoine Mattei; ⊙ 8.30am-8pm Mon-Sat, 10am-1pm & 2-4pm Sun Jun-Sep, shorter hours rest of year) Seriously hi-tech with no brochures, just monumental touch screens – everywhere. Sells tickets for guided tours and cultural events.

ARLES & THE CAMARGUE

Arles

POP 53,660

Arles' poster boy is the celebrated impressionist painter Vincent van Gogh. If you're familiar with his work, you'll be familiar with Arles: the light, the colours, the landmarks and the atmosphere, all of which he faithfully captured.

SWEET TREAT

Aix' sweetest treat since King René's wedding banquet in 1473 is the marzipan-like local speciality, *calisson d'Aix*, a small, diamond-shaped, chewy delicacy made on a wafer base with ground almonds and fruit syrup, and glazed with icing sugar. Traditional *calissonniers* still make them, including La Maison du Roy René (www.calisson.com; 13 rue Gaston de Saporta; ⊙ 9.30am-1pm & 2-6.30pm Mon-Sat, 9am-4pm Sun), which runs tours of its small factory on the city's fringe.

**TOP TIP:
VISIT
VENTABREN**

A lesser-known hilltop village, Ventabren (population 5000), 16km west of Aix, provides the perfect lazy-day detour. Meander sun-dappled cobbled lanes, peep inside a 17th-century church, and take in panoramic views of Provence from the ruins of Château de la Reine Jeanne before a superb lunch or dinner at La Table de Ventabren (☑04 42 28 79 33; www.latabledeventabren.com; 1 rue Cézanne; lunch menu Tue-Fri €40, 5-course tasting menu €89, mains from €28; ☺noon-1.15pm Wed-Sun, 7.45-9.15pm dinner Tue-Sun), which is reason enough to visit. The terrace looks out to distant mountains, magical on starry summer evenings. Michelin-starred chef Dan Bessoudo creates inventive, wholly modern French dishes and knockout desserts. Reservations essential.

But long before Van Gogh rendered this grand Rhône River locale on canvas, the Romans valued its worth. In 49 BC Arles' prosperity and political standing rose meteorically when it backed a winner in Julius Caesar (who would never meet defeat in his entire career). After Caesar plundered Marseille, which had supported his rival Pompey the Great, Arles eclipsed Marseille as the region's major port. Within a century and a half, it boasted a 12,000-seat theatre and a 20,000-seat amphitheatre to entertain its citizens with gruesome gladiatorial spectacles and chariot races.

Still impressively intact, the two structures now stage events including Arles' famous *férias* (bull-running festivals), with their controversial lethal bullfights, the less bloody *courses camarguaises* (the Camargue version) and three days of street parties.

Contrasting dramatically with Arles' ancient history is its increasingly dynamic, contemporary art scene – reflected in the 2014 opening of the new, state-of-the-art Fondation Vincent Van Gogh and the future 2018 opening of an arts centre for the Luma Foundation (http://luma-arles.org). The flamboyant, aluminium twist of a building, designed by world-renowned architect Frank Gehry no less, will become the centrepiece

of Parc des Ateliers, a rejuvenated industrial area next to the train station once abuzz with railway hangars and workshops.

◉ Sights & Activities

Les Arènes   Roman Site

(Amphithéâtre; adult/child incl Théâtre Antique €6.50/5; ☺9am-7pm) Slaves, criminals and wild animals (including giraffes) met their dramatic demise before a jubilant 20,000-strong crowd during Roman gladiatorial displays at Les Arènes, built around the early 2nd century AD. During the early medieval Arab invasions the arch-laced circular structure – 136m long, 107m wide and 21m tall – was topped with four defensive towers. By the 1820s, when the amphitheatre was returned to its original use, 212 houses and two churches had to be razed on the site.

Buy tickets for bloody bullfights, bloodless *courses camarguaises,* theatre and concerts at the ticket office next to the entrance.

★ Fondation Vincent Van Gogh   Museum

(☑04 90 49 94 04; www.fondation-vincent vangogh-arles.org; 33 ter rue du Docteur Fanton; adult/child €9/4; ☺11am-7pm, to 9pm Thu) This Van Gogh–themed gallery is a must-see, as much for its contemporary architecture and design, as for the art it showcases. It has no permanent art collection; rather, it hosts one or two temporary exhibitions a year, always with a Van Gogh theme and always including at least one Van Gogh masterpiece. Architectural highlights include the rooftop terrace and the kaleidescope-style bookshop 'ceiling' aka chunks of coloured glass forming a roof.

★ Musée Réattu   Museum

(☑04 90 49 37 58; www.museereattu.arles.fr; 10 rue du Grand Prieuré; adult/child €7/free; ☺10am-6pm Tue-Sun, to 5pm Dec-Feb) This splendid modern-art museum is housed in the exquisitely renovated 15th-century Grand Priory of the Knights of Malta. Among its collections are works by 18th- and 19th-century Provençal artists and two paintings and 57 sketches by Picasso. It hosts wonderfully curated cutting-edge exhibitions.

Musée Départemental Arles Antique   Museum

(☑04 13 31 51 03; www.arles-antique.cg13.fr; av de la Première Division Française Libre; adult/child €8/5;

⊙10am-6pm Wed-Mon) This striking, state of-the-art cobalt-blue museum perches on the edge of what used to be the Roman chariot racing track (circus), 1.5km southwest of the tourist office. The rich collection of pagan and Christian art includes stunning mosaics and an entire wing dedicated to archaeological treasures evoking Arles' commercial and navigation past.

Théâtre Antique
Roman Site

(☑ 04 90 96 93 30; bd des Lices; adult/child €6.50/free, with Les Arènes admission free; ⊙9am-7pm May-Sep, shorter hours rest of year) Still used for summertime concerts and plays, this outdoor theatre dates to the end of the 1st century BC. For hundreds of years it was a source of construction materials, with workers chipping away at the 102m-diameter structure (the column on the right-hand side near the entrance indicates the height of the original arcade). Enter on rue de la Calade.

Église & Cloître St-Trophime
Church, Cloister

(place de la République; church free, cloister adult/child €3.50/free; ⊙9am-7pm May-Sep, shorter hours rest of year) Arles was an archbishopric from the 4th century until 1790, and this Romanesque-style church was once a cathedral. Built in the late 11th and 12th centuries, it's named after St Trophime, an Arles bishop from the 2nd or 3rd century AD. On the western portal, the intricately sculpted tympanum depicts St Trophime holding a spiral staff. Inside, the treasury contains bone fragments of Arles' bishops. Occasional exhibitions are hosted in neighbouring cloister, Cloître St-Trophime.

Les Alyscamps
Cemetery

See p22.

Thermes de Constantin
Roman Site

See p22.

Place du Forum
Roman Site

(Cryptoportiques; adult/child €3.50/free; ⊙cryptoportiques 9am-noon & 2-7pm May-Sep, shorter hours rest of year) Just as social, political and religious life revolved around the forum in Roman Arles so this busy plane-tree-shaded square buzzes with cafe life today. Underneath it lie the underground galleries of Cryptoportiques – the forum's subterranean foundations and buried arcades (the plaza was lower in Roman times) carved out, 89m long and 59m wide, in the 1st century BC. Access is from the Hôtel de Ville on place de la République.

Les Arènes, Arles

PROVENCE ARLES

Arles

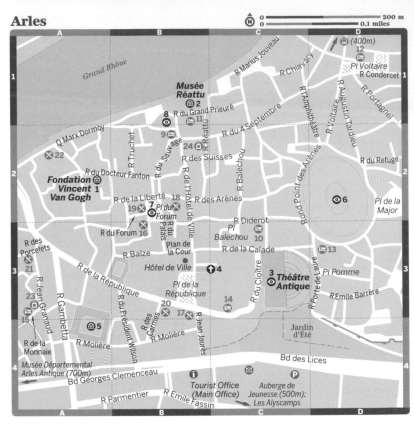

Arles

◉ Top Sights

1	Fondation Vincent Van Gogh	A2
2	Musée Réattu	B1
3	Théâtre Antique	C3

◉ Sights

4	Église & Cloître St-Trophime	C3
5	Espace Van Gogh	A4
6	Les Arènes	D2
7	Place du Forum	B2
8	Thermes de Constantin	B1

🛏 Sleeping

9	Hôtel Arlatan	B2
10	Hôtel de l'Amphithéâtre	C3
11	Hôtel du Musée	B1
12	Le Belvédère Hôtel	D1

13	Le Calendal	D3
14	Le Cloître	C3
15	L'Hôtel Particulier	A3

✴ Eating

16	Chez Caro	B3
17	Comptoir du Sud	B3
18	Fad'Ola	B2
19	Glacier Arlelatis	B2
20	L'Atelier	B3
21	Le Gibolin	A3
22	L'Entrevue	A2

🛍 Shopping

23	La Botte Camarguaise	A3
24	La Boutique des Passionnés	B2

Espace Van Gogh
Gallery

(📞04 90 49 39 39; place Félix Rey) The former hospital where Van Gogh had his ear stitched and was later locked up – not to be confused with the asylum Monastère St-Paul de Mausole (p41) – hosts the occasional exhibition. Other times, its small courtyard garden is worth a peek.

✯ Festivals & Events

Féria d'Arles
Bullfighting

(Féria de Pâques; www.feriaarles.com; ☉ Easter) Festival heralding the start of bullfighting season, with bullfighting in Les Arènes most Sundays in May and June.

Fête des Gardians
Cultural Festival

(☉1 May) Mounted Camargue cowboys parade and hold games during this festival.

Les Suds
Music Festival

(www.suds-arles.com; ☉ Jul) Vibrant world-music festival, held over one week in early July.

Les Rencontres d'Arles Photographie
Art Festival

(www.rencontres-arles.com; ☉ early Jul-Sep) International photography festival.

Féria du Riz
Bullfighting

(www.feriaarles.com; ☉ Sep) Bullfights during this week-long festival mark the start of the rice harvest.

🛏 Sleeping

Arles has reasonably priced, excellent year-round accommodation, which only really fills during *férias;* some hotels only open April to October. Hotels' private parking tends to be pricey.

★ Hôtel de l'Amphithéâtre
Historic Hotel €

(📞04 90 96 10 30; www.hotelamphitheatre.fr; 5-7 rue Diderot; s/d/tr/q €61/79/129/139; ❄ @ 🛜) Crimson, chocolate, terracotta and other rich earthy colours dress the exquisite 17th-century stone structure of this stylish hotel, with narrow staircases, a roaring fire and alfresco courtyard breakfasts. The romantic suite has a dreamy lilac-walled terrace overlooking rooftops. Breakfast €8.50.

Le Belvédère Hôtel
Boutique Hotel €

(📞04 90 91 45 94; www.hotellebelvedere-arles.com; 5 place Voltaire; s €65, d €70-90; ❄ 🛜) This sleek 17-room hotel is one of the best Arlésian pads. Red-glass chandeliers (and friendly staff) adorn the lobby breakfast area and the superclean rooms and bathrooms are fitted out in stylish red, chocolate brown and grey. Breakfast €7.50.

Hôtel du Musée
Boutique Hotel €

(📞04 90 93 88 88; www.hoteldumusee.com; 11 rue du Grand Prieuré; s/d/tr/q from €60/70/95/120; ☉mid-Mar-Oct; ❄ 🛜) In a fine 17th- to 18th-century building, this impeccable hotel has comfortable rooms, a checkerboard-tiled breakfast room and a sugar-sweet patio garden brimming with pretty blossoms. Breakfast €8.50, parking €10.

Auberge de Jeunesse
Hostel €

(📞04 90 96 18 25; www.fuaj.org; 20 av Maréchal Foch; dm incl breakfast & sheets €18.50; ☉mid-Feb–mid-Dec, reception closed 10am-5pm) This sunlit place, made up of eight-bed dorms, is 10 minutes' walk from the centre. Its bar closes at 11pm, just like its gates (except during *férias*).

★ Le Cloître
Design Hotel €€

(📞04 88 09 10 00; www.hotel-cloitre.com; 18 rue du Cloître; s/d €100/125; @ 🛜) Unbeatable value, the Cloister – 12th-century neighbour to the Cloître St-Trophime – is the perfect fusion of historic charm and contemporary design. Its 19 rooms across two floors tout high ceilings, bold colours and a funky mix of patterns and textures. Breakfast (€13), served in the wonderfully airy and 1950s-styled breakfast room, is a particularly stylish affair. No elevator. Free bike rental.

There is no lovelier way to end the day than with an *apéro* (aperitif) on the chic rooftop terrace, privy to wonderful views of the sculpted stone façade of the St-Trophime cloister.

★ Le Calendal
Hotel €€

(📞04 90 96 11 89; www.lecalendal.com; 5 rue Porte de Laure; s €66-99, d €99-130, tr €119-149, q €149-199; ☉lunch noon-2.30pm, salon de thé 4-6pm) Overlooking the Théâtre Antique, this bright hotel is a wonderful spot to stay. Rooms have beamed ceilings and bright Provençal fabrics, but the real heart-stealers are the spa Au Bain du Calendal and the lush flowery garden with terrace cafe Le Comptoir du Calendal. No summer breakfast (€12, open

VINCENT VAN GOGH

Vincent van Gogh was only 37 when he died. Born in 1853, the Dutch painter arrived in Arles in 1888 after living in Paris with his younger brother Theo, an art dealer who financially supported Vincent from his own modest income.

Revelling in Arles' intense light and bright colours, Van Gogh painted with a burning fervour. During the howling mistral (wind) he would kneel on his canvases and paint horizontally, or lash his easel to iron stakes driven deep into the ground. He sent paintings to Theo to sell, and dreamed of founding an artists' colony in Arles, but only Gauguin followed up his invitation. Their differing artistic approaches (Gauguin believed in painting from imagination, Van Gogh painting what he saw) and their artistic temperaments came to a head with the argument in December 1888 that led to Van Gogh lopping off part of his own ear.

In May 1889 Van Gogh voluntarily entered an asylum, Monastère St-Paul de Mausole (p41) in St-Rémy de Provence, 25km northeast of Arles over the Alpilles, where he painted 150-odd canvases, including *Starry Night* (not to be confused with *Starry Night over the Rhône*, painted in Arles). In February 1890, his 1888 work *The Red Vines*, painted in Arles, was bought by Anne Boch, sister of his friend Eugene Boch, for 400 francs (around €50 today) – the only painting he sold in his lifetime. It now hangs in the Pushkin State Museum of Fine Arts.

On 16 May 1890 Van Gogh moved to Auvers-sur-Oise, near Paris, to be closer to Theo. But on 27 July he shot himself. He died two days later with Theo at his side. Theo subsequently had a breakdown, was committed and died, aged 33, six months after Vincent. Less than a decade later, Van Gogh's talent started to achieve recognition, with major museums acquiring his work.

Van Gogh painted some 200 canvases in Arles and there is always at least one displayed in the Fondation Vincent Van Gogh. Van Gogh's little 'yellow house' on place Lamartine, painted in 1888, was destroyed during WWII. Mapped out in a tourist office brochure (€1 or downloadable for free online), the evocative Van Gogh walking circuit of the city takes in scenes painted by the artist.

to nonguests too), lunch or afternoon drink in Arles is more peaceful than here.

Hôtel Arlatan
Historic Hotel €€

(04 90 93 56 66; www.hotel-arlatan.fr; 26 rue du Sauvage; d €85-157; mid-Mar–mid-Nov;) The heated swimming pool, pretty garden and plush rooms decorated with antique furniture are just some of the things going for this hotel. Add to that a setting steeped in history, with Roman foundations visible through a glass floor in the lobby and 15th-century paintings on one of the lounges' ceilings. Breakfast continental/buffet €9/15.

L'Hôtel Particulier
Boutique Hotel €€€

(04 90 52 51 40; www.hotel-particulier.com; 4 rue de la Monnaie; d from €309; Easter-Oct) This exclusive boutique hotel with restaurant, spa and hammam (Turkish steam bath) oozes chic charm. From the big black door with heavy knocker to the crisp white linens and minimalist decor, everything about this 18th-century private mansion enchants.

✖ Eating

Arles' Saturday-morning market fills the length of bd des Lices with stalls of Camargue salt, goat-milk cheese and *saucisson d'Arles* (bull-meat sausage). The scene shifts to bd Émile Combes on Wednesday morning.

No town square is more crammed with cafe pavement terraces than Roman place du Forum, an inevitable stop of any Van Gogh walking tour thanks to the famously bright yellow façade of tourist-rammed Café Van Gogh, thought to be the cafe painted by Van Gogh in his *Café Terrace at Night* (1888).

Several hip, shabby-chic cafes bespeck rue des Porcelets and surrounding streets in the increasingly trendy and edgy Roquette *quartier*. When it all gets too much, seek out the floral peace and tranquility of the garden café at Le Calendal hotel.

Fad'Ola
Sandwiches €

(☑ 04 90 49 70 73; 40 rue des Arènes; sandwiches €3.80-6.50, salads €4.50-15; ☺ 11.30am-3pm & 7-10pm, shorter hours low season) Well-stuffed sandwiches – made to order, *frotté à l'ail* (rubbed with garlic) and dripping with silken AOC Vallée des Baux olive oil – lure crowds to this sandwich shop with a hole-in-the-wall takeaway counter. It also sells olive oil by the litre (€12 to €25). Find it footsteps from central 'cafe' square, place du Forum.

Glacier Arlelatis
Ice Cream €

(8 place du Forum; 1/2 scoops €2/4; ☺ 12.30-11pm) Creamy, delicious artisanal ice-cream is the mainstay of this *glacier* (ice creamery) on busy place du Forum. Buy a cone to takeaway or treat yourself to a magnificent whipped-cream-topped sundae sitting down. Flavours change but there's always a few distinctly Provençal ones: lavender honey, chestnut and so forth.

Comptoir du Sud
Cafe €

(☑ 04 90 96 ?? 17; 2 rue Jean Jaurès; sandwiches €4.10-5.70; ☺ 9am-6pm Tue-Fri) Gourmet sandwiches, wraps and bagels (tasty chutneys, succulent meats, foie gras) and divine little salads are served at this stylish *épicerie fine* (gourmet grocery). Take away or eat in on bar stools and end with a sweet €3 wedge of homemade *clafoutis* (cherry pie) for dessert.

L'Entrevue
Moroccan €

(☑ 04 90 93 37 28; www.lentrevue-restaurant.com; place Nina Berberova; mains €14-23; ☺ noon-2pm & 7.30-10.30pm; 🅿) Excellent heaped terracotta *tians* (bowls) of organic tajines and couscous are briskly served quayside at this colourful address, just around the corner from the Fondation Vincent Van Gogh.

Chez Caro
Bistro €€

(☑ 04 90 97 94 38; www.chezcaro.fr; 12 place du Forum; 2-/3-course menu €29/36; ☺ noon-2pm & 8-10pm Thu-Mon) Discreetly set at the far end of place du Forum, dwarfed by the imposing façade of the Nord Pinus hotel, Chez Caro is a modern bistro with vintage school furniture and some of Arles' finest modern French cooking. Wannabe alfresco diners can plump for a table on the bijou pavement terrace or – less appealing – with the masses in the middle of the square.

Salami on display at an outdoor market, Arles

A BULLISH AFFAIR

Not all types of bullfights end with blood. The Camargue variation, the *course camarguaise*, sees amateur *razeteurs* (cowboys, from the word for 'shave'), wearing skin-tight white shirts and trousers, get as close as they dare to the *taureau* (bull) to try to snatch rosettes and ribbons tied to the bull's horns, using a *crochet* (a razor-sharp comb) held between their fingers. Their leaps over the arena's barrier as the bull charges are spectacular.

Bulls are bred on a *manade* (bull farm) by *manadiers*, helped in their daily chores by *gardians* (Camargue cattle-herding cowboys). These mounted herdsmen parade through Arles during the Fête des Gardians on 1 May. Otherwise spend a morning with a herd of them at the Manade des Baumelles (☎ 04 90 97 84 14; www.manadedesbaumelles.com; D38; bull-farm tour with/without lunch €45/25), a bull farm south of Arles in the Camargue countryside where you can learn about farm life and bull breeding, and watch cowboys at work in the field from the safety of a tractor-pulled truck. Tours end with an optional farm lunch. Find the *manade* a few kilometres north of Stes-Maries-de-la-Mer, at the end of a gravel track off the D38 towards Aigues-Mortes.

Many *manades* also breed the creamy white *cheval de Camargue* (Camargue horse).

A calendar of *courses camarguaises* during the bullfighting season (Easter to September) is online at the Fédération Française de la Course Camarguaise (French Federation of Camargue Bullfights; ☎ 04 66 26 05 35; www.ffcc.info); several are held in Stes-Maries-de-la-Mer.

★ **Le Gibolin**   Bistro €€

(☎ 04 88 65 43 14; 13 rue des Porcelet; menus €27-32, glass wine €4.50-5.50; ⊙12.15-2pm & 8-10pm Tue-Sat Sep-Jul) Sup on peerless home cooking (think cod with fennel confit and crushed potatoes, pot au feu), while the friendly patroness bustles between dark-wood tables sharing her knowledge and passion for natural wines at Arles' most beloved *bar à vins nature* (wine bar). Pairings are naturally *magnifique*. No credit cards.

L'Atelier   Gastronomic €€€

(☎ 04 90 91 07 69; www.rabanel.com; 7 rue des Carmes; lunch menus €65 & €110, dinner menus €125 & €185; ⊙sittings begin noon-1pm & 8-9pm Wed-Sun) Consider this not a meal, but an artistic experience (with two shiny Michelin stars no less). Every one of the seven or 13 edible works of art is a wondrous composition of flavours, colours and textures courtesy of charismatic chef Jean-Luc Rabanel. Many products are sourced from the chef's organic veggie patch and wine pairings are an adventure in themselves. Also offers half-day cooking classes (with/without lunch €200/145).

🛍 Shopping

La Botte Camarguaise   Shoes

(☎ 06 16 04 08 14; 22 rue Jean Granaud; ⊙9am-12.30pm & 2-6.30pm Mon-Fri, 7am-noon Sat) Buy handmade Camargue-style cowboy boots.

La Boutique des Passionnés   Music

(☎ 04 90 96 59 93; www.passionnes.com; 14 rue Réattu; ⊙9am-7pm Tue-Sat) Gig flyers, tickets and music by Roma bands at this specialist music shop, also known as 'Musiques Arles'.

ℹ Information

Tourist Office (Main Office) (☎ 04 90 18 41 20; www.tourisme.ville-arles.fr; esplanade Charles de Gaulle; ⊙9am-6.45pm Apr-Sep, to 4.45pm Mon-Fri & 12.45pm Sun Oct-Mar)

ℹ Getting Around

Europbike Provence (☎ 06 38 14 49 50; www.europbike-provence.net; per day adult €10-18, child €8, electric e-bike €35; ⊙8am-6pm) Rents bikes of all shapes and sizes, for adults and kids, plus trailers for kids (€5 per day), kids' seats (€3 per day) and GPS units (€7 per day). Before setting off, download suggested cycling itineraries from Europbike's website.

Camargue Countryside

Just south of Arles, Provence's rolling landscapes yield to the flat, marshy wilds of the Camargue countryside, famous for its teeming bird life, roughly 500 species. King of all is the pink flamingo, which enjoys the expansive wetlands' mild winters. Equally famous are the Camargue's small white horses; their mellow disposition makes horse riding the ideal way to explore the region's patchwork of salt pans and rice fields, and meadows dotted with grazing bulls. Bring your binoculars – and some mosquito repellent.

Enclosed by the Petit Rhône and Grand Rhône Rivers, most of the Camargue wetlands fall within the 850-sq-km Parc Naturel Régional de Camargue, established in 1970 to preserve the area's fragile ecosystems while sustaining local agriculture. On the periphery, the Étang de Vaccarès and nearby peninsulas and islands form the Réserve Nationale de Camargue, a 135-sq-km nature reserve.

The Camargue's two largest towns are the seaside pilgrim's outpost Stes-Maries-de-la-Mer and, to the northwest, the walled town of Aigues-Mortes.

◉ Sights & Activities

Musée de la Camargue　　　　Museum
(Musée Camarguais; ☑04 90 97 10 82; www.parc-camargue.fr; Mas du Pont de Rousty, D570; adult/child €5/free, 1st Sun & last Wed of month free; ☒9am-12.30pm & 1-6pm Wed-Mon Apr-Oct, 10am-12.30pm & 1-5pm Nov-Mar) Inside a 19th-century sheep shed 10km southwest of Arles, this museum evokes traditional local life: exhibitions cover history, ecosystems, farming techniques, flora and fauna. *L'Oeuvre Horizons* by Japanese artist Tadashi Kawamata – aka a wooden observatory shaped like a boat – provides a bird's-eye view of the agricultural estate, crossed by a 3.5km walking trail. The headquarters of the Parc Naturel Régional de Camargue are also based here.

**Parc Ornithologique
du Pont de Gau**　　　　Bird Park
See p45.

★ Domaine de la Palissade　　　　Nature Park
See p46.

Les Cabanes de Cacharel　　　　Horse Riding
(☑04 90 97 84 10, 06 11 57 74 75; www.cabanesdecacharel.com; rte de Cacharel; 1/2/3hr horse trek €20/30/40) Farms along route d'Arles (D570) offer *promenades à cheval* (horseback riding) astride white Camargue horses, but a more authentic experience can be had at these stables, just north of Stes-Maries-de-la-Mer along the parallel rte de Cacharel (D85A). Horse-and-carriage rides too (€15 for one hour).

Absolut Kiteboarding　　　　Water Sports
(☑06 88 15 10 93; www.absolutkiteboarding.fr; 36 rte d'Arles, Salin de Giraud; group/private lesson €130/300) Ride the waves and the wind with this recommended kitesurfing school, headed by Patrick. March to November you're on the water, December to February on dry ground. The school runs a shop and rents gear (€70). Find it at the northern entrance to Salin-de-Giraud, on the D36.

⊨ Sleeping

★ Cacharel Hotel　　　　Hotel €€
(☑04 90 97 95 44; www.hotel-cacharel.com; rte de Cacharel, D85A; s/d/tr/q €128/140/152/173, horse-riding per hour €30; @ 🛜 🏊 🐾) This isolated farmstead, 400m down an unpaved track off the D85A just north of Stes-Maries-de-la-Mer, perfectly balances modern-day comforts with rural authenticity. Photographic portraits of the bull herder who created the

---

VIEW TO A THRILL

No view is wilder or more soul-stirring than the sweep of salt pans, salt mountains and diggers at work that unfolds 2km south of the village of Salin de Giraud, along the D36D. Park in the car park, just before the 'slag heaps' of harvested salt, and trek up to the windwept **Point de Vue** (viewpoint) to gorge on a stunning panorama of pink-hued *salins* (salt pans). Europe's largest, they produce 800,000 tonnes of salt per year.

The next 12km south along this same road to the Domaine de la Palissade (p46) passes pink flamingos wading through water and is equally unforgettable.

hotel in 1947 (son Florian runs the three-star hotel with much love today) give the vintage dining room soul and rooms sit snug in whitewashed cottages, some overlooking the water.

Swings in the paddock, horse-riding with a *gardian* (cowboy), boules to play *pétanque* and bags of open space between fig trees and pines make it a perfect family choice. Cacharel is one of the few Camargue hotels to open year-round.

★ Mas de Calabrun   Hotel €€

(☎04 90 97 82 21; www.mas-de-calabrun.fr; rte de Cacherel, D85A; d/roulotte €129/169; ☺mid-Feb–mid-Nov; @ 🤶 🏊 🐎) From the striking equestrian sculpture in its front courtyard to the swish pool, stylish restaurant terrace and fabulous views of open Camargue countryside, this hotel thoroughly deserves its three stars. The icing on the cake however is its trio of *chic roulottes* (old-fashioned 'gypsy' wagons) which promise the perfect romantic getaway. Breakfast buffet €15.

Le Mas de Peint   Boutique Hotel €€€

(☎04 90 97 20 62; www.masdepeint.com; Le Sambuc; d from €260, menus €59 & €97; ☺mid-Mar–mid-Nov; 🕸 🤶 🏊) So chic and gentrified it almost feels out of place in the Camargue, this upmarket *mas* (farmhouse) – part of the luxurious Châteaux & Hôtels Collection – is right out of design mag *Côte Sud*. The good news: nonguests are welcome in its gourmet restaurant and swish, poolside canteen.

✕ Eating

★ La Telline   Camarguais €€

(☎04 90 97 01 75; www.restaurantlatelline.fr; rte de Gageron, Villeneuve; mains €23-32.50; ☺lunch & dinner Fri-Mon) A true local favourite, this isolated cottage restaurant with sage-green wooden shutters could not be simpler or more authentic. Summer dining is in a small and peaceful, flower-filled garden; and the no-frills *menu* cooks up a straightforward choice of *tellines* (baby squid), salad or terrine as starter followed by grilled fish or meat, or a beef or bull steak. No credit cards.

Chez Bob   Carmarguais €€

(☎04 90 97 00 29; http://restaurantbob.fr; Mas Petite Antonelle, rte du Sambuc, Villeneuve; menu €45; ☺noon-2pm & 7.30-9pm Wed-Sun) This house restaurant is an iconic address adored by Arlesians. Feast on grilled bull chops, duck breasts and lamb beneath trees or inside between walls plastered in photos, posters and other memorabilia collected over the years by Jean-Guy alias 'Bob'. Find his pad 20km south of Arles in Villeneuve, 800m after the crossroads on the D37 towards Salin. Reserve online.

★ La Chassagnette   Gastronomic €€€

(☎04 90 97 26 96; www.chassagnette.fr; rte du Sambuc; 6-course menu with/without wine €180/125, mains €35-38; ☺noon-1.30pm & 7-9.30pm Thu-Mon Apr-Jun, Sep & Oct, daily Jul & Aug, Thu-Sun Nov-Mar) Inhaling the scent of sun-ripened tomatoes is one of many pleasures at this 19th-century sheepfold – the ultimate Camargue dining spot. Alain Ducasse prodigy Armand Arnal cooks up a 100% organic *menu,* grows much of it himself and woos guests with a mosquito-protected outside terrace. Look for the fork and trowel sign, 12km southeast of Arles on the southbound D36, just north of Le Sambuc.

Stes-Maries-de-la-Mer

POP 2422

You could be forgiven for thinking you'd crossed into Spain at this remote seaside outpost, where whitewashed buildings line dusty streets and dancers in bright dresses spin flamenco. During its Roma pilgrimages, street-cooked pans of paella fuel chaotic crowds of carnivalesque guitarists, dancers and mounted cowboys.

◉ Sights & Activities

Tickets for bullfights at Stes-Maries' Arènes are sold at the beachfront arena, from where 30km of golden-sand beaches – easily reached by bicycle or on foot – lace the shoreline east and west.

Église des Stes-Maries   Church

(www.sanctuaire-des-saintesmaries.fr; place Jean XXIII; adult/child €2.50/1.50; ☺10am-noon & 2-5pm Mon-Sat, 2-5pm Sun) This 12th- to 15th-century church, with its dark, hushed, candle-wax-scented atmosphere, draws legions of Roma pilgrims to venerate the statue of black Sara, their revered patron saint, during the Pèlerinage des Gitans. The relics of Sara and those of Marie-Salomé and Marie-Jacobé, all found in the crypt by King René in 1448, are

THE STORY OF THE MARYS & GITAN PILGRIMAGES

Catholicism first reached European shores in tiny Stes-Maries-de-la-Mer. The tale goes that Saints Marie-Salomé (Mary Salome) and Marie-Jacobé (Mary of Clopas) – and some say Mary Magdalene – fled the Holy Land in a little boat and were caught in a storm, drifting at sea until washing ashore here.

Provençal and Catholic lore diverge at this point: Catholicism relates that Sara, patron saint of the *gitans* (Roma Gitano people), travelled with the two Maries (Marys) on the boat. Provençal legend says Sara was already here and was the first person to recognise their holiness. In 1448, skeletal remains said to belong to Sara and the two Marys were found in a crypt in Stes-Maries-de-la-Mer.

Gitans make a pilgrimage, Pèlerinage des Gitans, here on 24 and 25 May, dancing, playing music and parading a statue of Sara through town. The Sunday in October closest to the 22nd sees a second pilgrimage dedicated to the two Saint Marys (Stes Maries); *courses camarguaises* (Camargue-style bullfights)are also held at this time.

enshrined in a wooden chest, stashed in the stone wall above the choir. Don't miss the panorama from the rooftop terrace (€2).

★ Digue à la Mer
Dike, Cycling

This 2.5m-high dike was built in the 19th century to cut the delta off from the sea. A 20km-long walking and cycling track runs along its length linking Stes-Maries with the solar-powered Phare de la Gacholle (1882), a lighthouse automated in the 1960s. Footpaths cut down to lovely sandy beaches and views of pink flamingos strutting across the marshy planes are second to none. Walking on the fragile sand dunes is forbidden.

Le Vélo Saintois
Cycling

(☑ 04 90 97 74 56; www.levelosaintois.camargue.fr; 19 rue de la République; per day adult/child €15/13.50, tandem €30; ☻ 9am-7pm Mar-Nov) This bike-rental outlet has bikes of all sizes, including tandems and kids' wheels. Helmets cost an extra €1 per day and a free brochure details four circular cycling itineraries (26km to 44km, four hours to eight hours) starting in Stes-Maries-de-la-Mer. It also offers half-day biking and paddle-board/beach-sailing packages (€35/40). Free hotel delivery.

Le Vélociste
Cycling

(☑ 04 90 97 83 26; www.levelociste.fr; place Mireille; per day adult/child €15/13.50; ☻ 9am-7pm Mar-Nov) This bike-rental shop rents wheels, advises on cycling itineraries (24km to 70km, four hours to nine hours) and organises fun one-day cycling/horse riding or cycling/canoeing packages (€30). Free hotel delivery.

Boating
Water Sports

The marshy Camargue lends itself to exploration by boat (adult/child €12/6 per 90-minute trip). Several companies including Les Quatre Maries (☑ 04 90 97 70 10; www.bateaux-4maries.camargue.fr; 36 av Théodore Aubanel; ☻ mid-Mar–Oct) and Le Camargue (☑ 06 17 95 81 96; http://bateau-camargue.com; 5 rue des Launes; ☻ mid-Mar–Oct) have ticketing desks along rue Théodore Aubanel in the promenade linking the town centre with Port Gardian. Further west past the pleasure port, next to Camping Le Clos du Rhône, is Tiki III (☑ 04 90 97 81 68; www.tiki3.fr; ☻ mid-Mar–mid-Nov), a paddle boat moored at the mouth of the Petit Rhône.

For canoeing and kayaking on the Petit Rhône, contact Kayak Vert Camargue (☑ 04 66 73 57 17; www.kayakvert-camargue.fr; Mas de Sylvéréal), 14km north of Stes-Maries off the D38.

- - - - - - - - - - - - - - - - - -

🛏 Sleeping

★ Hôtel Méditerranée
Hotel €

(☑ 04 90 97 82 09; www.hotel-mediterranee. camargue.fr; 4 av Frédéric Mistral; s/d/tr/q €50/65/75/90, d with shower €45; ☻ mid-Mar–mid-Nov; ✳) This white-washed cottage hotel, festooned with an abundance of flower pots steps from the sea, is truly a steal. Its 14 rooms – three with their own little terrace garden – are spotlessly clean, and breakfast is served in summer on a pretty vine-covered patio garden – equally festooned with strawberry plants, germaniums and other potted flowers. Breakfast €7. Bike rental €15 per day.

SUR LA PLAGE

Lunch *sur la plage* (on the beach) never fails to seduce and Stes-Maries-de-la-Mer lives up to the promise with two hip 'n' dandy beach restaurants, both open May to September.

Heading east towards the Digue à la Mer on sandy **Plage Est** is **La Playa** (☑ 06 29 48 82 01; www.laplaya-en-camargue.fr; Plage Est; mains €17-20; ☺ 8am-midnight May-Sep), the chic choice, with a particularly vibrant *apéro* (apertif) and after-dark scene, shoals of fresh fish cooked up *à la plancha* (grilled), and great daytime buzz revolving around tasty lunches, free wi-fi and super-comfy sunloungers on the sand.

In the opposite direction, on equally sandy **Plage Ouest**, is **Calypso** (☑ 07 71 03 43 46; av Riquette Aubanel, Plage Ouest; fish & shellfish platters €12-16, mains €19.50-23; ☺ 10am-7pm May-Sep, to 11pm Sat Jul & Aug), shaded by a typical reed pergola with picture-postcard lookout to sea. Feast on good-value bowls of *moules* (mussels) around tables on its elevated wooden-decking terrace, then rent a sunlounger (€12) for a sand-side siesta.

Camping Le Clos du Rhône
Campground €

(☑ 04 90 97 85 99; www.camping-leclos.fr; rte d'Aigues Mortes; tent, car & two adults €26.50; ☺ Apr-Oct; 🅿 🛜 ♨ 🐕) Right by the beach, this large and well-equipped campsite sports the whole range of accomodation options: tent pitches, wooden chalets, self-catering cottages. The pool with two-lane water slide and a beachside spa with jacuzzi and hamman make it a real family-favourite.

⭐ Lodge Sainte Hélène
Boutique Hotel €€

(☑ 04 90 97 83 29; www.lodge-saintehelene.com; chemin Bas des Launes; d €130-173; ✳ @ 🛜 ♨) These designer-chic, pearly-white terraced cottages strung along a lake edge are prime real estate for bird-watchers and romance seekers. Each room comes with a bird-spotters' guide and binoculars, and dynamic owner Benoît Noel is a font of local knowledge. Breakfast €15.

✕ Eating

⭐ La Cabane aux Coquillages
Seafood €

(☑ 06 10 30 33 49; www.degustationcoquillages-lessaintesmariesdelamer.com; 16 av Van Gogh; mains €16.50-21.50; ☺ noon-3pm & 5-11pm Mar-Nov) The shellfish-*apéro* arm of neighbouring Ô Pica Pica, this bright blue 'shack' with crates of crustaceans piled high inside and a gaggle of sea-blue chairs outside is pure gold. Wash down half a dozen oysters (€6.50), locally harvested *tellines* (€12.50) or your choice of *fritures* (deep-fried and battered baby prawns, baby squid or anchovies, €12.50) with a glass of chilled white, and enter nirvana.

⭐ Ô Pica Pica
Seafood €

(☑ 06 10 30 33 49; www.degustationcoquillages-lessaintesmariesdelamer.com; 16 av Van Gogh; ☺ noon-3pm & 7-11pm Mar-Nov) Fish and shellfish does not come fresher than this. Watch it gutted, filleted and grilled in the 'open' glass-walled kitchen, then devour it on the sea-facing pavement terrace or out back in the typically Mediterranean white-walled garden. Simplicity is king here: plastic glasses, fish and shellfish platters, no coffee and no credit cards.

La Casita
Camarguais €€

(☑ 04 86 63 63 14; 3 rue Espelly; mains €19-28; ☺ noon-3pm & 7-11pm Apr–mid-Nov) The charismatic couple who run this unpretentious address with cartwheels for tables cook up the catch of the day for eight months of the year, and spend the other four travelling. The result: local dishes such as *tellines,* cooked *à la plancha* and spiced with a tasty pinch of chilli, cumin or other world flavour.

La Grange
Provençal €€

(☑ 04 90 97 98 05; 23 av Frédéric Mistral; mains €15-29, menus €18.50 & €29.50; ☺ noon-2pm & 6.30-10pm Mar-Nov) Throw yourself into local cowboy culture at the Grange, an ode to the Camargue's guardian with bull-herding memorabilia on the walls and plenty of *taureau* (bull meat) on the menu. Portions are copious, making the fixed *menus* excellent value for feisty appetites. Kickstart the experience with a Lou Gardian, the house *apéro* mixing white wine and peach liqueur.

ℹ Information

Tourist Office (☑ 04 90 97 82 55; www.saintesmaries.com; 5 av Van Gogh; ☺ 9am-7pm)

STES-MARIES-DE-LA-MER

This silvery chain of low, jagged mountains, strung between the rivers Durance and Rhône, delineate a *très chic* side of Provence, notably around upmarket St-Rémy-de-Provence, known for fine restaurants and summertime celebrity spotting. The entire region is chock-a-block with gastronomic delights – AOC olive oil, vineyards, Michelin-starred restaurants and truffles. History comes to life at magnificent ruined castles, remnants of medieval feuds, and at one of Provence's best Roman sites, the ancient city of Glanum.

St-Rémy de Provence

POP 11,033

See-and-be-seen St-Rémy has an unfair share of gourmet shops and restaurants – in the spirit of the town's most famous son, prophecy-maker Nostradamus, we predict you'll add a notch to your belt. Come summer, the jet set hits the Wednesday market, wanders the peripheral boulevard and congregates on place de la République, leaving the quaint historic centre strangely quiet.

◉ Sights

Pick up a Carte St-Rémy at the first sight you visit, get it stamped, then benefit from reduced admission at the second sight.

Site Archéologique
de Glanum
Roman Site

(☑ 04 90 92 23 79; http://glanum.monuments-nationaux.fr; rte des Baux-de-Provence; adult/child €7.50/free, parking €2.70; ⊙ 9.30am-6.30pm Apr-Sep, 10am-5pm Oct-Mar, closed Mon Sep-Mar) Spectacular archaeological site Glanum dates to the 3rd century BC. Walking the main street towards the sacred spring around which Glanum grew, you pass fascinating city remains: baths, forum, marketplace, temples and houses. Two ancient Roman monuments – a triumphal arch (AD 20) and mausoleum (30 to 20 BC) – mark the entrance, 2km south of St-Rémy.

Monastère St-Paul
de Mausole
Historic Site

(☑ 04 90 92 77 00; www.cloitresaintpaul-valetudo.com; adult/child €4.65/3.30; ⊙ 9.30am-7pm Apr-Sep, 10.15am-5.15pm Oct-Mar) Van Gogh admitted himself to Monastère St-Paul de Mausole in 1889. The asylum's security led to his most productive period – he completed 150-plus drawings and some 150 paintings here, including his famous *Irises*. A reconstruction of his room is open to visitors, as are the gardens and Romanesque cloister that feature in several of his works. From the monastery entrance, a walking trail is marked by colour panels, showing where the artist set up his easel. St-Paul remains a psychiatric institution: an exhibition room sells artwork created by patients.

🛏 Sleeping

Hôtel Canto Cigalo
Hotel €

(☑ 04 90 92 14 28; www.cantocigalo.com; 8 chemin Canto Cigalo; d €74-97; ✳ @ 🛜 ☒) This excellent-value 20-room hotel with apricot façade and blue wooden shutters is a 10-minute stroll from town. Simple and clean, its frilly, feminine rooms are decorated in dusty rose, with wicker and white-wood furniture. Unusually, guests have the choice of a gluten/lactose-free breakfast (€10.50) as well as regular *petit-déj* (€9) with homemade bread and jam. South-facing rooms have air-con.

★ Sous les Figuiers
Boutique Hotel €€

(☑ 04 32 60 15 40; www.hotel-charme-provence.com; 3 av Gabriel St-René Taillandier; d €96-122; tr €186; ✳ @ 🛜 🐾) A five-minute walk from town, this country-chic house hotel has 14 art-filled rooms facing a leafy garden – lovely

Site Archéologique de Glanum
MARTIN CHILD/GETTY IMAGES ©

for unwinding after a day's explorations. The owner is a painter (who runs half-day classes costing €85 per person) and has exquisite taste, marrying design details such as velvet and distressed wood, Moroccan textiles, and rich colour palates. Breakfast €13.50.

✕ Eating

Maison Cambillau   Boulangerie €

(1 rue Carnot; fougasses & sandwiches €2.60-3; ⊘7.30am-1.30pm & 3-7.30pm Fri-Wed) Well-stuffed *fougasse* (Provençal flatbread) and baguette sandwiches with a variety of tasty fillings make this boulangerie the perfect spot to stock up on a picnic. Complete the takeaway feast with a feisty meringue, bag of nougat, nutty florentine or almond- and pistachio-studded *crousadou*.

Les Filles du Pâtissier   ·   Cafe €

(📋06 50 61 07 17; 3 place Favier; mains €15-20; ⊘10am-10pm, closed Wed Apr-Oct) Particularly perfect on sultry summer nights, this upbeat and colourful cafe has vintage tables filling one corner of a delightful car-free square in the old town. Its daily-changing *menu* features market-driven salads and tarts, and come dusk it morphs into a wine bar with charcuterie plates and occasional live music. Don't miss the homemade *citronnade* and melon fizz soda.

SWEET RETREAT

Few addresses are as quintessentially Provençal as **Mas de l'Amarine** (📋04 90 94 47 82; www.mas-amarine. com; Ancienne voie Aurélia; d €190-270, 2-/3-course lunch menu €29/35, dinner mains €36), a sweet retreat to eat and sleep, five minutes east of town by car. Contemporary artwork fills this fashion-forward *auberge* (inn), a romantic old *mas* (farmhouse) and 1950s artist retreat, with traditional drystone walls, great old fireplace and funky Fatboy beanbags by the pool. Many of the ingredients cooked in the restaurant kitchen – open to nonguests too – come fresh from the magnificent gardens. Reservations well in advance are naturally essential.

Da Peppe   Italian €

(📋04 90 92 11 56; 2 av Fauconnet; pizza €13.50-15, pasta €14-21, mains €16.50-22; ⊘noon-2.30pm & 7-11pm Wed-Mon; 🖼) First-class pizzas cooked to Italian perfection by Sicilian chef Maurizio in a state-of-the-art wood-fuelled oven and a fabulous rooftop terrace with town and church views are two of the many draws of this new kid on the block. Da Peppe's volumunous interior is industrial-styled, with a funky bar covered in coffee-bean sacks to have a drink while waiting for a table.

La Cuisine des Anges   Bistro €€

(📋04 90 92 17 66; www.angesetfees-stremy.com; 4 rue du 8 Mai 1945; menu €28, mains €18-21; ⊘noon-2.30pm & 7.30-11pm Mon, Wed, Sat & Sun, 7.30-11pm Thu & Fri; ✿🐾) Packed in equal measure with locals and tourists, this casual *maison d'hôte* (B&B) has been around for an age and just does not lose its edge. Light Provençal dishes are derived from organic local ingredients and are served in the interior patio or wood-floored dining room with textured paintings and zinc-topped tables. Upstairs is cute-as-a-button B&B Le Sommeil des Fées (📋04 90 92 17 66; www.angesetfees-stremy.com; 4 rue du 8 Mai 1945; r incl breakfast €74-94), with five rooms.

★ Maison Druout   Modern French €€€

(📋04 90 15 47 42; http://maisondrouot.blogspot.fr; 150 rte de Maillane, D5; menus lunch €23-49, dinner €45-65; ⊘12.30-2.30pm & 7.30-11pm Wed-Sun) Snug in a 19th-century oil mill with a terrace basking in the shade of a fig tree and vine-covered pergola, this restaurant is pure style. Contemporary Provençal cuisine – made strictly from local products (listed in the *menu*) – is served with a creative twist in a thoroughly modern interior.

Find the mill-restaurant five minutes out of town, opposite supermarket Intermarché on the D5 towards Maillane.

🛍 Shopping

Espace Anikado   Boutique

(http://anikado.canalblog.com; 1 bd Marceau; ⊘10am-7pm) Immerse yourself in the vibrant local art, craft and design scene at this one-stop shop. Eye-catching, colourful and oozing creativity, the hybrid boutique-gallery showcases fashion, jewellery, shoes, furniture and more by local designers. Regular exhibitions by Provençal artists are held here, plus artsy events and happenings.

❶ Information

Tourist Office (☑ 04 90 92 05 22; www.
saintremy-de-provence.com; place Jean Jaurès;
⊙ 9.15am-12.30pm & 2-6.45pm Mon-Sat, 10am-
12.30pm Sun Jul & Aug, shorter hours rest of
year)

Orange

POP 30,008

Considering how exceptional Orange's Roman theatre is (if you see only one Roman
site in France, make it this one), the ultra-
conservative town is surprisingly untouristy,
and eerily quiet in winter. Accommodation
is good value, compared with swankier
towns such as Avignon, but it's nearly im-
possible to find an open restaurant on Sunday or Monday night.

The House of Orange, the princely dynas-
ty that ruled Orange from the 12th century,
made its mark on the history of the Netherlands through a 16th-century marriage
with the German House of Nassau, and then
English history through William of Orange.
Orange was ceded to France in 1713 by the
Treaty of Utrecht. To this day, many mem-
bers of the royal house of the Netherlands
are known as the princes and princesses of
Orange-Nassau.

◉ Sights

★ Théâtre Antique   Roman Site
(www.theatre-antique.com; rue Madeleine Roch;
adult/child €9.50/7.50; ⊙ 9am-7pm Jul & Aug, to
6pm Apr, May & Sep, to 5.30pm Mar & Oct, 9.30am-
4.30pm rest of year) Orange's Roman theatre
is France's most impressive Roman site. Its
sheer size and age are awe-inspiring: designed for 10,000 spectators, it's believed to
have been built during Augustus Caesar's
rule (27 BC to AD 14). The 103m-wide, 37m-
high stage wall is one of three in the world
still standing in entirety (others are in Syria
and Turkey) – minus a few mosaics, plus a
new roof. Admission includes an audioguide
and access to Musée d'Art et d'Histoire, opposite the theatre.

Musée d'Art et d'Histoire   Museum
(www.theatre-antique.com; Rue Madeleine Roch;
adult/child €5.50/4.50; ⊙ 9.15am-7pm Jun-Aug,
to 6pm Apr, May & Sep, shorter hours rest of year)
This small museum – free admission with
a Théâtre Antique ticket – displays various
unassuming treasures, including portions

✓ **TOP TIP:
ROMAN PASS**

Excellent value is the combo **Roman
Pass** (adult/child €18/13.50), valid for
seven days and covering admission to
all the Roman sights in both Orange and
Nîmes in neighbouring Languedoc. Buy
it at any Roman venue in either town.

of the Roman survey registers (precursor to
the tax department) and friezes that once
formed part of the Roman theatre's scenery.

Arc de Triomphe   Roman Site
See p24.

Colline St-Eutrope   Gardens
See p24.

⌕ Sleeping

Hôtel l'Herbier d'Orange   Hotel €
(☑ 04 90 34 09 23; www.lherbierdorange.com;
8 place aux Herbes; s/tr/q €55/71/81, d €59-76;
❄@◈📶) Friendly, enthusiastic owners
keep this small, basic hotel looking spick
and span, with double-pane windows and
gleaming bathrooms. Find it sitting prettily
on on a small square shaded by tall plane
trees. Breakfast is a choice of continental
(€6) or buffet (€9).

Hôtel Arène   Hotel €€
(☑ 04 90 11 40 40; www.hotel-arene.fr; place de
Langes; d €116-150, annexe €60-80; ❄@◈⊠📶)
It might be part of the generic Best Western chain, but the Arène is beautifully po-
sitioned in the old town and retains some
individuality. Kids love the two heated pools
(one indoors, one out); parents appreciate
the family-size rooms. Request a remodelled
room in the main building – cheaper rooms
in the annexe are older.

Hôtel Le Glacier   Hotel €€
(☑ 04 90 34 02 01; www.le-glacier.com; 46 cours
Aristide Briand; d €58-195; ❄@◈) All 28 rooms
are individually decorated and impeccably
maintained by the charming owners, who
pay attention to detail. There's easy parking
in front of the hotel, and bike rental. Breakfast is €10.

Vaison-la-Romaine

🍴 Eating

It's worth wandering away from the cafe terraces opposite the Théâtre Antique on place des Frères Mounet to delve into the pedestrian squares of Orange's softly hued old town where a multitude of dining and drinking spots await beneath leafy plane trees.

Market stalls spill across streets in the town centre every Thursday.

À la Maison   Bistro €

(☑ 04 90 60 98 83; 4 place des Cordeliers; menus 2-/3-course lunch €12.50/15, dinner €25/32; ◷ noon-2pm & 7-10pm Mon-Sat) There's no lovelier spot on a warm night than the leafy courtyard, wrapped around an old stone fountain and a trio of plane trees, at this simple bistro across from the walls of the Théâtre Antique. Its name 'At Home' is a perfect reflection of the cuisine it serves.

Au Salon de Charlotte   Tearoom €

(4 place Clemenceau; breakfast/brunch €6.50/10, mains €12; ◷ 8am-7pm Wed-Sun) This delightful *salon de thé* is deliciously old-fashioned with its floral tablecloths and vases of freshly cut flowers on each table. Its organic teas, homemade cakes, lunchtime tarts and

Sunday brunch are just as delicious. Find it next to the Hôtel de Ville on car-free place Clemenceau.

El Camino Store   Cafe €

(☑ 04 88 84 49 99; 8 rue Notre Dame; ◷ 8am-7pm Tue-Sat) *Tintin* books, dial-up telephones, Corgi model cars and old Playmobil figurines are among the vintage collectibles strewn around this cool, 1950s-styled cafe. Food – strictly homemade – is limited to one starter and one main. Savour it inside around formica tables or outside on the flowery pavement terrace.

Les Artistes   Bistro, Cafe €

(place de la République; 1-/2-/3-course menu €11/13.50/15.50; ◷ 8am-2am) A hybrid drinking/dining address with a chic contemporary interior and vast pavement terrace on a pedestrian old-town square, the Artists buzzes from dawn to dark. Happy Hour (5pm to 8pm) is great value, as are its meal-sized salads and other brasserie fare.

La Grotte d'Auguste   Traditional French €€

(☑ 04 90 60 22 54; www.restaurant-orange.fr; rue Madeleine Roch, Théâtre Antique; lunch/dinner menu €21/28, mains €20; ◷ noon-2pm & 7-10pm Tue-Sat) Location is key at Auguste's Grotto, squirrelled away in the entrails of Orange's Roman theatre. Summer dining overlooks the ruins of a 2nd-century Hemicycle temple. Cuisine is traditional French, with lots of meat cuts and gourmet treats such as foie gras and black truffles.

Le Parvis Gastronomic €€
(☑ 04 90 34 82 00; www.restaurant-le-parvis-orange. com; 55 cours Pourtoules; menus 2-/3-course lunch €23/29, dinner €36/46; ⊙ lunch & dinner Tue-Sat, lunch Sun) Nobody speaks above a whisper at Orange's top table where chef Jean-Michel Bérengier has cooked up superb Provençal food for the past 25 years.

❶ Information

Tourist Office (☑ 04 90 34 70 88; www.otorange. fr; 5 cours Aristide Briand; ⊙ 9am-6.30pm Mon-Sat, to 1pm & 2-6.30pm Sun, closed Sun Oct-Mar)

Vaison-la-Romaine

POP 6036

Tucked between seven hills, Vaison-la-Romaine has long been a traditional exchange centre, and still has a thriving Tuesday market. The village's rich Roman legacy is very visible and 20th-century buildings rise alongside France's largest archaeological site. A Roman bridge crosses the Ouvèze River, dividing the contemporary town's pedestrianised centre and the walled, cobbled-street hilltop Cité Médiévale – one of Provence's most magical ancient villages, where the counts of Toulouse built their 12th-century castle. Vaison is a good base for jaunts into the Dentelles de Montmirail and Mont Ventoux, but tourists throng here in summer: reserve ahead.

◉ Sights

Gallo-Roman Ruins Roman Site
See p25.

Cité Médiévale Historic Quarter
Cross the Pont Romain (Roman bridge) in the footsteps of frightened medieval peasants, who clambered to the walled city during valley conflicts. Steep cobblestone alleyways wend beneath stone ramparts and a 14th-century bell tower past romantic fountains and mansions with incredibly carved doorways. Continue uphill to the 12th-century château and be rewarded with eagle-eye vistas.

Festival & Events

Choralies Music Festival
(www.choralies.fr) Europe's largest choral festival is held in August every three years. Upcoming festivals will be held in 2016 and 2019.

Festival des Chœurs Lauréats Music Festival
(www.festivaldeschoeurslaureats.com; ⊙ late Jul) The best choirs in Europe.

⏨ Sleeping

★ Hôtel Burrhus Hotel €
(☑ 04 90 36 00 11; www.burrhus.com; 1 place de Montfort; d €64-94, apt €140; ❋ 🛜) On Vaison's vibrant central square, this blue-shuttered hotel is quaint and old from the outside and brilliantly contemporary inside, with original art works and sculptures strung in its enchanting maze of vintage corridors and staircases. Don't miss the giant Roman-inspired terracota pot, 1.8m tall, suspended between rooftops above the sofa-clad interior patio. No lift. Breakfast €9.

L'École Buissonière B&B €
(☑ 04 90 28 95 19; www.buissonniere-provence.com; D75, Buisson; s €49-54, d €62-74, tr €78-89 q €94-99; 🛜) Five minutes north of Vaison, in the countryside between Buisson and Villedieu, hosts Monique and John have transformed their stone farmhouse into a tastefully decorated three-bedroom B&B, big on comfort. Breakfast features homemade jam, and there's an outdoor summer kitchen.

ART OF THE MATTER

Be inspired by contemporary art fest Supervues (www.supervues.com), hosted each December by Hôtel Burrhus. For three days, usually midmonth, the hotel's 38 rooms are taken over by artists from all over Europe who each create a work of art or installation in the room they're sleeping in. The hotel is closed to guests, but anyone can visit during the day to watch the artists at work.

L'Évêché
B&B €€

(☑ 04 90 36 13 46; http://eveche.free.fr; rue de l'Évêché; s/d/tr from €85/93/120) With groaning bookshelves, vaulted ceilings, higgledy-piggledy staircase, intimate salons and exquisite art, this five-room *chambre d'hôte*, in the medieval city, is fabulously atmospheric. Knowledgable owners Jean-Loup and Aude also lend bikes.

Hostellerie Le Beffroi
Historic Hotel €€

(☑ 04 90 36 04 71; www.le-beffroi.com; rue de l'Évêché; d €76-120, tr €150-216; ☺ Apr-Jan; 🛜) Within the medieval city's walls, this *hostellerie*, dating from 1554, fills two buildings (the 'newer' one was built in 1690). A fairy-tale hideaway, its rough-hewn stone-and-wood-beamed rooms are small, but romantic, and its restaurant opens onto a rose-and-herb garden with kids' swings.

✗ Eating

Maison Lesage
Boulangerie €

(2 rue de la République; sandwiches €4-6; ☺ 7am-1pm & 3-5pm Mon, Tue & Thu-Sat, to 1pm Sun) Generously stuffed baguette sandwiches, artisanal caramels and nougat, cakes, pastries and bun-sized meringues in a rainbow of flavours makes this busy bakery near the tourist office a top stop for picnic fodder (best savoured by the water on the pebbly river banks – follow the grassy path from the 'Cité Médievale Pont Romain' car park).

★ Bistro du'O
Neobistro €€

(☑ 04 90 41 72 90; rue du Château; menus €24-45; ☺ noon-2pm & 7.30-10pm Mon, Tue & Thu-Sat) No address seduces more than this thoroughly modern gastro-bistro squirrelled away in a 13th-century vaulted cellar in the medieval city. Dynamic couple Gaëlle (front of house) and Philippe (chef) have been the creative duo behind the address since summer 2013 and local seasonal produce is their muse. Fussy eaters note the choice of dishes is short (but superb) – a perfect reflection of what's at the market that day.

Le Moulin à Huile
Gastronomic €€€

(☑ 04 90 36 20 67; www.moulin-huile.com; quai Maréchal Foch, rte de Malaucène; menus lunch €39, dinner €59 & €69, mains €35-48; ☺ noon-2pm & 7.30-10pm Tue-Sat, to 2pm Sun) Michelin-starred Chef Robert Bardot showcases gastronomic prowess in a former olive-oil mill with baby-blue wooden shutters by the river. Lunch on a simple truffle omelette (€55). In summer dine outside in the peachy garden, steps from the river (go for the upper terrace rather than lower one with plastic chairs). You can also make a night of it in one of three handsome guestrooms (€140-160).

ℹ Information

Tourist Office (☑ 04 90 36 02 11; www.vaison-ventoux-tourisme.com; place du Chanoine Sautel; ☺ 9.30am-noon & 2-5.45pm Mon-Sat year-round, plus 9.30am-noon Sun mid-Mar–Oct)

Mont Ventoux & Around

Visible for miles around, Mont Ventoux (1912m), nicknamed *le géant de Provence* (Provence's giant), stands like a sentinel over northern Provence. From its summit, accessible by road between May and October (the white glimmering stuff you see in summer are *lauzes,* broken white stones, not snow), vistas extend to the Alps and, on a clear day, the Camargue.

Because of the mountain's dimensions, every European climate type is present on its slopes, from Mediterranean on its lower southern reaches to Arctic on its exposed northern ridge. As you ascend the relentless gradients (which regularly feature in the Tour de France), temperatures can plummet by 20°C, and there's twice as much precipitation as on the plains below. The relentless mistral wind blows 130 days a year, sometimes at a speed of 250km/h. Bring warm clothes and rain gear, even in summer.

This climatic patchwork is reflected in the mountain's diverse fauna and flora, now actively protected by Unesco Biosphere Reserve status.

Piercing the sky to the west of Mont Ventoux are the spectacular limestone pinnacles of another walker's paradise, Dentelles de Montmirail. On the other side of the Dentelles sits the snug village of Beaumes de Venise, home to France's finest muscat; the village tourist office (☑ 04 90 62 94 39; www.ot-beaumesdevenise.com; place du Marché, Beaumes de Venise; ☺ 9am-noon & 2-7pm Mon-Sat, shorter hours rest of year) has details of local vineyards.

Three principal gateways – Bédoin, Malaucène and Sault – provide services in summer, but they're far apart.

You can reach Mont Ventoux by car from Sault via the D164; or (summer only) from Malaucène or St-Estève via the D974, often blocked by snow until April.

Mont Ventoux

🏃 Activities

Walking

The GR4 crosses the Dentelles de Montmirail before scaling Mont Ventoux' northern face, where it meets the GR9. Both traverse the ridge. The GR4 branches eastwards to Gorges du Verdon; the GR9 crosses the Vaucluse Mountains to the Luberon. The essential map for the area is *3140ET Mont Ventoux*, by IGN (www.ign.fr). Bédoin's tourist office (p84) stocks maps and brochures detailing walks for all levels.

In July and August, tourist offices in both Bédoin and Malaucène facilitate night-time expeditions up the mountain to see the sunrise (over 15 years only).

Cycling

Tourist offices distribute *Les Itinéraires Ventoux*, a free map detailing 11 itineraries – graded easy to difficult – highlighting artisanal farms en route. For more cycling trails, see www.lemontventoux.net.

At Station Ventoux Sud Bike Park (☎ 04 90 61 84 55; www.facebook.com/VentouxBikePark; Chalet Reynard; half-/full day €14/10; ☺ 10am-5pm Sat & Sun, weekday hours variable), near the summit, mountain-bikers ascend via a rope tow (minimum age 10 years), then descend ramps and jumps down three trails (total length 5km), from beginner to advanced. Bring your own bike, helmet and full-length gloves or rent all the gear at Chalet Reynard. Bédoin Location (☎ 04 90 65 94 53; www.bedoin-location.fr; 20 rte Malaucène, Bédoin; rental per half-/full day from €15/20; ☺ Mar-Nov), opposite the tourist office in Bédoin, also rents equipment and delivers to the summit.

ℹ️ Information

Every village in the area has a tourist office and the following resources are also handy:
Destination Ventoux (www.destination-ventoux.com)

Provence Cycling (www.provence-cycling.com)

Provence des Papes (www.hautvaucluse.com)

Bédoin Tourist Office (☑ 04 90 65 63 95; www.bedoin.org; Espace Marie-Louis Gravier, Bédoin; ☺ 9am-12.30pm & 2-6pm Mon-Sat, 9.30am-12.30pm Sun mid-Jun–Aug) Excellent source of information on all regional activities; also helps with lodging.

Malaucène Tourist Office (☑ 04 90 65 22 59; http://villagemalaucene.free.fr; place de la Mairie, Malaucène; ☺ 9.15am-12.15pm & 2.30-5.30pm Mon-Fri, 9am-noon Sat) Stocks info on Mont Ventoux, but (surprisingly) not the Dentelles.

Sault Tourist Office (☑ 04 90 64 01 21; www.saultenprovence.com; av de la Promenade, Sault; ☺ 9am-noon & 2-5pm Mon-Sat) Good resource for Ventoux.

THE LUBERON

The picture-perfect area that makes up the Luberon is rectangular on a map, but navigating its bucolic rolling hills, golden-hued perched villages and hidden valleys is a bit like fitting together a jigsaw puzzle. The Luberon is named after its main mountain range, which is split in the centre by the Combe de Lourmarin, a beautiful narrow river valley. Luberon's hues, fragrances and flavours subtly transform in tune with the seasons.

PARC NATUREL RÉGIONAL DU LUBERON

Egyptian vultures, eagle owls, wild boars, Bonelli's eagles and Etruscan honeysuckle are among the species that call the 1650-sq-km Parc Naturel Régional du Luberon (www.parcduluberon.fr) home. Created in 1977 and recognised as a Biosphere Reserve by Unesco in 1997, the park encompasses dense forests, plunging gorges and 67 villages with a combined population of 155,000. The GR6, GR9, GR92 and GR97 walking trails all cross it, as does a 236km-long cycling route.

Pick up maps and guides at the Maison du Parc (☑ 04 90 04 42 00; www.parcduluberon.fr; 60 place Jean Jaurès; ☺ 8.30am-noon & 1.30-6pm Mon-Fri, 9am-noon Sat Apr-Sep, shorter hours rest of year) in Apt.

The region's capital, Apt, is a central hub for practicalities, but the heart of the Luberon is in the tiny stone villages fanning out across the countryside, which encompasses the Parc Naturel Régional du Luberon, the Abbaye Notre-Dame de Sénanque of postcard fame and ancient, stone *bories* (drywalled huts).

Apt

POP 12,422

Sleepy little Apt comes alive during its Saturday morning market brimming with local specialities, otherwise it's primarily a hub for shopping.

⊙ Sights

Musée de l'Aventure Industrielle du Pays d'Apt   Agricultural Museum

(Industrial History Museum; ☑ 04 90 74 95 30; 14 place du Postel; adult/child €4/free; ☺ 10am-noon & 2-6.30pm Mon-Sat, to 5.30pm Tue-Sat Oct-May) Gain an appreciation for Apt's artisanal and agricultural roots at this converted candied-fruit factory. The well-curated museum interprets the fruit and candying trade, as well as ochre mining and earthenware production from the 18th century.

Confiserie Kerry Aptunion   Sweets Factory

(☑ 04 90 76 31 43; www.lesfleurons-apt.com; Quartier Salignan, D900; ☺ 9am-12.15pm & 1.30-6pm Mon-Fri, to 12.15pm & 2-6pm Sat) **FREE** Thirty tonnes of cherries are candied daily at the Confiserie Kerry Aptunion, the world's largest crystallised-fruit factory, 2.5km west of town. Free tastings and guided tours; check the website for the seasonal schedule.

🛏 Sleeping

Hôtel le Palais   Budget Hotel €

(☑ 04 90 04 89 32; www.hotel-le-palais.com; 24bis place Gabriel-Péri; s/d/tr/q €45/55/65/80; 🕾🏠) Young, friendly owners lend a real air of dynamism to this veteran cheap-as-chips hotel. Breafast €5.

★ Le Couvent   B&B €€

(☑ 04 90 04 55 36; www.loucouvent.com; 36 rue Louis Rousset; d €95-130; 📧🕾📺) Behind a garden wall in the cobbled town centre, this enormous five-room *maison d'hôte* occupies a 17th-century former convent, and offers exceptional value and sense of place; breakfast is served in the old convent refectory.

Hôtel Sainte-Anne Hotel €€

(☑04 90 74 18 04; www.apt-hotel.fr; 62 place Faubourg-du-Ballet; d €92-123; 🔲@🛜) Lovely seven-room hotel in a 19th-century dwelling, completely renovated in 2010. Spotless, crisp-at-the-edges rooms mix modern and traditional furnishings, with exceptional beds and big bathtubs (though small toilets). Little extras include homemade jams and breads, made by the charming owner, served as part of the copious breakfasts (€10).

✖ Eating

L'Auberge Espagnole Tapas €

(http://laubergeespagnole-apt.com; 17 place au Sepier; tapas €4.50-8, lunch menu €13.50) Dominated by an ancient plane tree, the old-town square on which this colourful tapas bar spills could not be more enchanting – or typically Provençal. Take your pick from 22 different Spanish-inspired tapas chalked on the board, then sit at flowery tableclothed tables and savour the mellow scene.

Le Platane Modern French €€

(☑04 90 04 74 36; 25 place Jules Ferry; menus €15-30, mains €20; ☺noon-2.30pm & 7.30-10pm Tue-Sat; ☑) Everything is made from scratch at this simple, decent restaurant, which uses quality ingredients in its changing French *menus*. The leafy terrace is good on balmy nights.

❶ Information

Tourist Office (☑04 90 74 03 18; www.luberon-apt.fr; 20 av Philippe de Girard; ☺9.30am-1pm & 2.30-7pm Mon-Sat, to 12.30pm Sun) Excellent source of information for activities, excursions, bike rides and walks.

❶ Getting Around

Luberon Cycles (☑04 86 69 19 00; 86 quai Général-Leclerc; bike rental half-/full day from €12/16; ☺9am-noon & 2-6pm Mon-Sat)

North of Apt

Gordes & Around

Forming an amphitheatre over the rivers Sorgue and Calavon, the tiered village of Gordes (pop 2159) sits spectacularly on the white rock face of the Vaucluse plateau. In the early evenings the village is theatrically lit by the setting sun, turning the stone buildings a shimmering gold. Gordes has top billing on many tourists' must-see lists (particularly those of high-profile Parisians), so high season sees a cavalcade of coaches.

◉ Sights

**Abbaye Notre-Dame
de Sénanque** Church

See p29.

Village des Bories Architecture

(☑04 90 72 03 48; adult/child €6/4; ☺9am-8pm, shorter hours winter) Beehive-shaped *bories* (stone huts) bespeckle Provence and at the Village des Bories, 4km southwest of Gordes, an entire village of them can be explored. Constructed of slivered limestone, *bories* were built during the Bronze Age, inhabited by shepherds until 1839, then abandoned until their restoration in the 1970s. Visit early in the morning or just before sunset for the best light. Note the lower car park is for buses; continue to the hilltop car park to avoid hiking uphill in the blazing heat.

Musée de la Lavande Museum

(☑04 90 76 91 23; www.museedelalavande.com; Coustellet, D2; adult/child €6.80/free; ☺9am-7pm May-Sep, to noon & 2-6pm Oct-Apr) This museum, 7km south of Gordes in Coustellet, showcases top-end lavender. An audioguide and short video (in English) explain the lavender harvest, and giant copper stills reveal extraction methods. Guided tours depart at 1pm and 5pm daily May to September. The on-site boutique is an excellent (if pricey) one-stop shop for quality fine-lavender products, and there is a picnic area in the lavender-festooned garden (particularly pretty in summer when the lilac flower blooms).

🛏 Sleeping & Eating

⭐**Le Mas de la Beaume** B&B €€

(☑04 90 72 02 96; www.labeaume.com; rte de Cavaillon, Gordes; d €125-180; 🛜💺) In a visually stunning hilltop locale at the village's edge, this impeccable five-room *maison d'hôte* is like a Provençal postcard come to life, with yellow-washed stone-wall rooms decorated with bunches of lavender hanging from wood-beamed ceilings. Beds are dressed in

✓ TOP TIP: PICNIC PERFECT

Those short of time or money in *très cher* Gordes should follow the locals away from the main square and downhill along rue Baptistin Picca, to pocket-sized La Boulangerie de Mamie Jane (☑ 04 90 72 09 34; lunch menus €6.50 or €7.90; ⊘ 6.30am-1pm & 2-6pm Thu-Tue). In the same family for three generations, it is run with love and passion by retired sportsman-turned-*boulanger* Bob and his wife Valérie who cook up outstanding bread, pastries, cakes and biscuits (including purple, lavender-perfumed *navettes*). The well-filled baguette sandwiches (€4.50) and lunch *menus* comprising a sandwich/quiche, dessert and drink (€7.90/6.50) are unbeatable value.

high-thread-count linens, and breakfast is delivered to your room.

Mas de la Régalade   B&B €€

(☑ 04 90 76 90 79; www.masregalade-luberon.com; Quartier de la Sénancole, D2; d €120-150, dinner €36; ⊘ mid-Apr–mid-Nov; 🐾🎿) A stone farmhouse on a grassy plain surrounded by oak woodlands, 3.5km south of Gordes, Mas de la Régalade's four rooms artfully blend mod cons with playful antiques. In the garden, a vintage blue Citroën peeks between scented hedgerows of lavender and rosemary, beyond the big pool. Three times a week *table d'hôte* dinner is served.

Le Mas Tourteron   Gastronomic €€€

(☑ 04 90 72 00 16; www.mastourteron.com; chemin de St-Blaise les Imberts; menu €59; ⊘ 7.30-9.30pm Wed-Sat, 12.30-2pm & 7.30-9.30pm Sun Apr-Oct) The welcome is warm at this country house, surrounded by gardens clearly created with perfect lazy alfresco lunches in mind. The stone-walled dining room has a vaguely boho-chic feeling, befitting chef Elisabeth Bourgeois-Baique's stylised cooking. Husband Phillipe selects from more than 200 wines to pair with her seasonal, inventive *menus*. Desserts are legendary. It's 3.5km south of Gordes, off the D2.

ℹ Information

Tourist Office (☑ 04 90 72 02 75; www.gordes-village.com; place du Château; ⊘ 9am-noon & 2-6pm Mon-Sat, from 10am Sun) Inside Gordes' medieval château, which was enlarged and given its defensive Renaissance towers in 1525.

Roussillon

POP 1342

Some two millennia ago, the Romans used the ochreous earth around the spectacular village of Roussillon, set in the valley between the Plateau de Vaucluse and the Luberon range, for producing pottery glazes. These days the whole village, down to gravestones in the cemetery, is built of the reddish stone.

◉ Sights & Activities

Attractions focus on learning more about the region's signature ochreous earth. Roussillon's visual charms are no secret, so arrive early or late in the day.

★ Sentier des Ocres   Walking

(Ochre Trail; adult/child €2.50/free; ⊘ 9.30am-5.30pm; 🐾) In Roussillon village, groves of chestnut and pine surround sunset-coloured ochre formations, rising on a clifftop. Two circular trails, 30 or 50 minutes, twist through minidesert landscapes – it's like stepping into a Georgia O'Keeffe painting. Information panels highlight 26 types of flora to spot, the history of local ochre production, and so on. Wear walking shoes and avoid white!

Conservatoire des Ocres et de la Couleur   Museum

(Ochre & Colour Conservatory; ☑ 04 90 05 66 69; www.okhra.com; rte d'Apt; guided tours adult/student €6.50/5; ⊘ 9am-7pm Jul & Aug, to 6pm Sep-Jun, closed Mon & Tue Jan & Feb; 🐾) This arts centre and historic site examines all things pigment. Occupying a disused ochre factory (on the D104 east of Roussillon), it explores the properties of ochre through indoor-outdoor displays and artwork, fun for kids to run around. There's an excellent art and home-decor boutique stocking extensive ranges of powdered pigment. Two-hour workshops for adults (€19) and children (€11) explore different ways to use ochre in art. Tours year-round at 2.30pm and 3.30pm, plus 11am and 4.30pm in summer.

Mines de Bruoux
Historic Site

(☎ 04 90 06 22 59; www.minesdebruoux.fr; rte de Croagnes; adult/child €8.10/6.50; ☺10am-7pm Jul & Aug, to 6pm Apr-Jun, Sep & Oct) In Gargas, 7km east of Roussillon, this former ochre mine has spectacular spire-filled caves, like a serene mineral church. Visits are only by guided tour, check the schedule on the website; reservations required.

❶ Information

Tourist Office (☎ 04 90 05 60 25; www.roussillon-provence.com; place de la Poste; ☺9am-noon & 1.30-5.30pm Mon-Sat)

St-Saturnin-lès-Apt & Around

POP 2798

Tiny St-Saturnin-lès-Apt is refreshingly ungentrified and just beyond the tourist radar. It has a cafe, a bistro and empty cobbled streets that twist uphill from central square place de la Mairie to a rocky plateau crowned by château ruins and a high-in-the-sky church, still intact – from where the most fabulous panorama of the surrounding Vaucluse plateau unfolds. Pause along the rocky path to admire the craftsmanship behind the ancient drystone walls. Approach the village from Rustrel for an idyllic motor past pea-green vineyards and serried rows of lavender.

🛏 Sleeping & Eating

Le Saint Hubert
Hotel €

(☎ 04 90 75 42 02; www.hotel-saint-hubert-luberon.com; d €56-62, tr €72) Charm personified, this quintessential village *auberge* (inn) has welcomed travellers since the 18th century and is a gorgeous spot to stay. Rooms are simple but elegant, and the sweeping view of the southern Luberon from valley-facing rooms is breathtaking. Guests reluctant to stray too far can opt for half-board (€116 for two people) – dining on the panoramic terrace is no short straw. Breakfast €8.

Le Mas Perréal
B&B €€

(☎ 04 90 75 46 31; www.masperreal.com; Quartier la Fortune; s/d/tr incl breakfast €125/135/175; 🛜 ☒) Surrounded by vineyards, lavender fields and cherry orchards, on a vast 7-hectare property outside St-Saturnin-lès-Apt, this farmhouse B&B has five charmingly simple rooms, styled with country antiques and Provençal fabrics. Outside there's a heavenly pool and big garden with mountain views. Elisabeth, a long-time French teacher, offers cooking and French lessons (€30 per hour).

★La Coquillade
Hotel, Gastronomic €€€

(☎ 04 90 74 71 71; www.coquillade.fr; Le Perrotet, Gargas; lunch menus €38, dinner menus €72-115, d €325-390; ☺sittings 12.30-1.30pm & 7.30-9.30pm mid-Apr–mid-Oct) Overnighting at La Coquillade does not suit everyone's budget, unlike

the excellent-value lunch *menu* served in the casual bistro of this luxurious Relais & Châteaux hilltop estate with formal Michelin-starred restaurant. In July and August bistro dining moves into the Jardin de la Vignes, aka an enchanting outdoor patio overlooking a sea of vines. La Coquillade is 5km northwest of Apt, signposted uphill off the D900.

★ **La Table de Pablo** Modern French €€€

(☎04 90 75 45 18; www.latabledepablo.com; Les Petits Cléments, Villars; menus lunch €19 & €25, dinner €36 & €57, mains €22-26; ☺12.30-2pm & 7-10pm Mon, Tue, Fri & Sun, 7-10pm Thu & Sat) Its incongruous setting in a simple house near Villars is not momentous, but the cuisine and attitude of chef Thomas Gallardo are. From the basil grown on a Bonnieux farm to Forcalquier pigeon, cheese ripened by René Pellégrini and Luberon wine, everything is locally sourced. Top marks for the wine pairings. Children are welcomed with fruity cocktails and their own gastronomic *'petits bouts' menu* (€15).

NORTHEASTERN PROVENCE

Haute-Provence's heady mountain ranges arc across the top of the Côte d'Azur to the Italian border, creating a far-flung crown of snowy peaks and precipitous valleys. To the west, a string of sweet, untouristy hilltop villages and lavender fields drape the Vallée de la Durance. Magical Moustiers Ste-Marie is a gateway to the plunging white waters of Europe's largest canyon, the Gorges du Verdon. In the east, the Vallée des Merveilles wows with 36,000 Bronze Age rock carvings. In the far north are the winter ski slopes and summer mountain retreats of the Ubaye and Blanche Valleys. Outside of ski areas, many establishments close in winter.

Pays de Forcalquier

Beyond mass-tourism's radar, Pays de Forcalquier's expansive landscapes comprise wildflower-tinged countryside and isolated hilltop villages. At its heart atop a rocky perch sits its namesake, Forcalquier, a sleepy town that bursts into life once a week during its Monday-morning market. Steep steps lead to the gold-topped citadel and octagonal chapel atop the town.

Some 4km south of Forcalquier, outside the walled city of Mane, is perhaps Provence's most peaceful address: the 13th-century Prieuré de Salagon (☎04 92 75 70 50; www.musee-de-salagon.com; adult/child/family €7/5/20; ☺10am-8pm Jun-Aug, to 7pm May & Sep, to 6pm Oct–mid-Dec & Feb-Apr; ⊞) sits amid fields and five themed gardens, including a medieval herb garden, a show garden of world plants, and a wonderfully sweet-smelling Jardin des Senteurs (Garden of Scents) with much native lavender among the mints, mugworts and other fragant plants. Inside the old stone priory, a fascinating permanent exhibition explores lavender and its historical production, uses and culture in Haute-Provence. A stunning repertoire of seasonal concerts and temporary exhibitions – often including great art installations in the chapel – complete the enchanting ensemble.

Forcalquier's quaint pedestrian streets and squares have a generous sprinkling of restaurant terraces. The tourist office (☎04 92 75 10 02; www.forcalquier.com; 13 place du Bourguet; ☺9am-noon & 2-6pm Mon-Sat) has accommodation information.

Vallée de la Durance

At the western edge of Haute-Provence, the winding waters of the 324km-long Durance River, a tributary of the Rhône, follow the Via Domitia, the road from Italy that allowed the Romans to infiltrate the whole of France. Now it's the autoroute's path, a fast connector between the Alps and the coast.

Come summer, the area's highlight is the Plateau de Valensole, France's lavender capital. Cruise the plateau along the D6 or D8 for arresting views of unfolding purple ripples.

On the other side of the river, Monastère Notre Dame de Ganagobie (Ganagobie; ☺3-5pm Tue-Sun, shop 10.30am-noon & 2.30-6pm Tue-Sun) FREE, a 10th-century Benedictine monastery, is wonderful for a stroll among almond trees, beds of irises and quiet hilltop woods. The 12th-century floor mosaic (depicting dragons) inside the chapel is the largest of its kind in France, and a shop stocks monk-made soaps, honey and music. Ganagobie is signposted off the N96 between Lurs and Peyruis.

The French Riviera

With its glistening seas, idyllic beaches and fabulous weather, the Riviera (known as Côte d'Azur to the French) encapsulates many people's idea of the good life.

Although the Riviera does take beach-going *very* seriously – from nudist beach to secluded cove or exclusive club, there is something for everyone – the beauty is that there is so much more to do than just going to the beach.

Culture vultures will revel in the region's thriving art scene: the Riviera has some fine museums, including world-class modern art, and a rich history to explore in Roman ruins, WWII memorials and excellent museums.

Foodies for their part will rejoice at the prospect of lingering in fruit and veg markets, touring vineyards and feasting on some of France's best cuisines, while outdoor enthusiasts will be spoilt for choice with coastal paths to explore, and snorkelling and swimming galore.

History

The eastern part of France's Mediterranean coast, including the area now known as the Côte d'Azur, was occupied by the Ligurians from the 1st millennium BC. It was colonised around 600 BC by Greeks from Asia Minor, who settled along the coast in the areas of Massalia (present-day Marseille), Hyères, St-Tropez, Antibes and Nice. Called in to help Massalia against the threat of invasion by Celto-Ligurians from Entremont, the Romans triumphed in 125 BC. They created Provincia Romana – the area between the Alps, the sea and the Rhône River – which ultimately became Provence.

In 1388 Nice, along with the Haute-Provence mountain towns of Barcelonette and Puget-Théniers, was incorporated into the House of Savoy, while the rest of the surrounding Provençal region became part of the French kingdom in 1482. Following an agreement between Napoléon III and the House of Savoy in 1860, the Austrians were ousted and France took possession of Savoy.

Within the Provence–Alpes–Côte d'Azur *région,* the Côte d'Azur (or Riviera to Anglophones) encompasses most of the *départements* of the Alpes-Maritimes and the Var. In the 19th century, wealthy tourists flocked here to escape the northern winter, along with celebrated artists and writers, adding to the area's cachet. Little fishing ports morphed into exclusive resorts. Paid holidays for all French workers from 1936 and improved transportation saw visitors arrive in summer, making it a year-round holiday playground. But it's not all play, no work: since the late 20th century, the area inland of Antibes has been home to France's 'Silicon Valley', Sophia Antipolis, the country's largest industrial and technological hub.

Nice

POP 348,195

Nice offers exceptional quality of life: shimmering Mediterranean shores, the very best of Mediterranean food, a unique historical heritage and Alpine wilderness within an

 is not needed

Markets, Vieux Nice

hour's drive. No wonder so many young French people aspire to live here and tourists keep flooding in.

History

Nice was founded around 350 BC by the Greek seafarers who had settled Marseille. They named the colony Nikaia, apparently to commemorate a nearby victory (*nike* in Greek). In 154 BC the Greeks were followed by the Romans, who settled further uphill around what is now Cimiez, where there are still Roman ruins.

By the 10th century, Nice was ruled by the counts of Provence but turned to Amadeus VII of the House of Savoy in 1388. In the 18th and 19th centuries it was occupied several times by the French, but didn't definitively become part of France until 1860.

During the Victorian period, the English aristocracy and European royalty enjoyed Nice's mild winter climate. Throughout the 20th century, the city's exceptional art scene spanned every movement from impressionism to new realism. The tram line (customised by artists) and the decision to open all museums for free in 2008 show that art is still very much a part of city life.

◉ Sights

Nice has a number of world-class sights but the star attraction is probably the city itself: atmospheric, beautiful and photogenic, it's a wonderful place to stroll or watch the world go by, so make sure you leave yourself plenty of time to soak it all in.

◉ Vieux Nice

★ **Vieux Nice**   Historic Quarter
(☉ food markets 6am-1.30pm Tue-Sun) Nice's old town, a mellow-hued rabbit warren, has scarcely changed since the 1700s. Retracing its history – and therefore that of the city – is a highlight, although you don't need to be a history buff to enjoy a stroll in this atmospheric quarter. Vieux Nice is as alive and prominent today as it ever was.

Cue the cours Saleya: this joyous, thriving market square hosts a well-known flower market (☉ 6am-5.30pm Tue-Sat, to 1.30pm Sun) and a thriving fruit and vegetable market ☉ 6am-1.30pm Tue-Sun), a staple of local life. A flea market (☉ 8am-5pm Mon) takes over on Monday, and the spill over from bars and restaurants seems to be a permanent fixture.

Much of Vieux Nice has a similar atmosphere to cours Saleya, with delis, food shops, boutiques and bars crammed in its tiny lanes. Rue de la Boucherie and rue Pairolière are excellent for food shopping. You'll also find a fish market (☺6am-1pm Tue-Sun) at place St-François.

Much harder to spot because of the narrow lane it sits on is the baroque Palais Lascaris (15 rue Droite; guided visit €5; ☺10am-6pm Wed-Mon, guided tour 3pm Fri) FREE, a 17th-century mansion housing a frescoed orgy of Flemish tapestries, faience (tin-glazed earthenware) and gloomy religious paintings. On the ground floor is an 18th-century pharmacy.

Baroque aficionados shouldn't miss Nice's other architectural gems such as Cathédrale Ste-Réparate (place Rossetti), honouring the city's patron saint, or the exuberant Chapelle de la Miséricorde (cours Saleya).

Parc du Château   Garden

(☺8am-6pm in winter, to 8pm in summer) On a rocky outcrop towering over Vieux Nice, this park offers a cinematic panorama of Nice and the Baie des Anges on one side, and the port on the other. The 12th-century castle was razed by Louis XIV in 1706; only the 16th-century Tour Bellanda remains. It is a fabulous place for picnics. To get here, ride the free Château Lift (Ascenseur du Château; rue des Ponchettes; ☺9am-6pm winter, to 8pm summer) from beneath Tour Bellanda, or hike up from the old town or the port.

Other simple attractions include Cascade Donjon, an 18th-century artificial waterfall crowned with a viewing platform, and kids' playgrounds.

Port Lympia   Architecture

Nice's Port Lympia, with its beautiful Venetian-coloured buildings, is often overlooked, but a stroll along its quays is lovely, as is the walk to get here: come down through Parc du Château or follow quai Rauba Capeu, where a massive war memorial hewn from the rock commemorates the 4000 Niçois who died in both world wars.

◉ Cimiez

Cimiez used to be the playground of European aristocrats wintering on the Riviera. These days, it's Nice's affluent residents who live in the area's beautiful Victorian villas.

Musée Matisse   Art Museum

(www.musee-matisse-nice.org; 164 av des Arènes de Cimiez; ☺10am-6pm Wed-Mon) FREE Located about 2km north of the centre in the leafy quarter of Cimiez, the Musée Matisse houses a fascinating assortment of works by Matisse that document the artist's stylistic evolution, including oil paintings, drawings, sculptures, tapestries and Matisse's signature famous paper cut-outs. The permanent collection is displayed in a red-ochre 17th-century Genoese villa overlooking an olive-tree-studded park. Temporary exhibitions are hosted in the futuristic basement building. Sadly, all explanations are in French only.

Matisse lived nearby in the 1940s, in the monumental Régina building at 71 bd de Cimiez. Originally Queen Victoria's wintering palace, it had been converted and Matisse had two apartments that he used as his home and studio. He died here in 1954 and is now buried at the cemetery of the Monastère de Cimiez (place du Monastère; ☺8.30am-12.30pm & 2.30-6.30pm), across the park from the museum.

Musée National Marc Chagall   Art Museum

(www.musee-chagall.fr; 4 av Dr Ménard; adult/child €8/6; ☺10am-5pm Wed-Mon Oct-Jun, to 6pm Jul Sep) This small museum houses the largest public collection of works by Belarusian painter Marc Chagall (1887-1985). The main hall contains 12 huge interpretations (1954-67) of stories from Genesis and Exodus. In an antechamber, an unusual mosaic of Elijah in his fiery chariot, surrounded by signs of the zodiac, is viewed through a plate-glass window and reflected in a small pond. The

---

ℹ INFO: FRENCH RIVIERA PASS

Although most museums in Nice are free, there are still plenty of attractions that you have to pay for in Nice and along the Riviera. The French Riviera Pass (www.frenchrivierapass.com; 1-/2-/3-day pass €26/38/56) includes access to a number of these sights. It is available online or at the Nice tourist office.

Attractions within Nice that are included in the price of the pass are the Musée National Marc Chagall, Nice Le Grand Tour bus and guided walking tours.

Nice

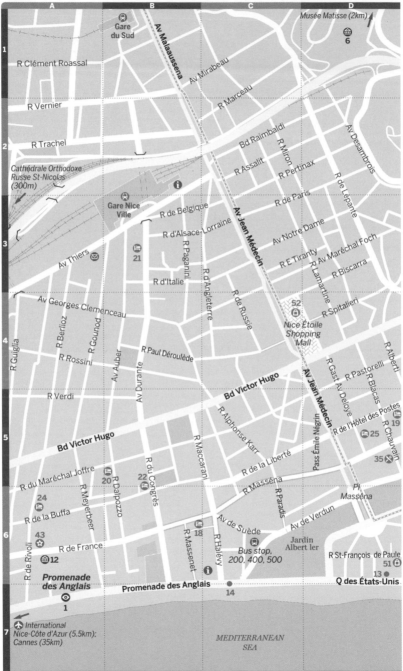

Gare du Sud

Av Malaaussena

Musée Matisse (2km)

6

R Clément Roassal

Av Mirabeau

R Marceau

R Vernier

R Trachel

Bd Raimbaldi

R Miron

R Pertinax

Av Desambrois

R Assalit

Cathédrale Orthodoxe
Russe St-Nicolas
(300m)

R de Lépante

R de Paris

Gare Nice
Ville

R de Belgique

Av Jean Médecin

Av Notre Dame

R d'Alsace-Lorraine

R E Tiranty

Av Maréchal Foch

Av Thiers

21

R Paganini

R Lamartine

R Biscarra

R d'Italie

R d'Angleterre

R de Russie

R Spitalieri

Av Georges Clemenceau

52

Nice Étoile
Shopping
Mall

R Berlioz

R Gounod

R Rossini

R Paul Déroulède

Av Jean Médecin

R Alberti

R Guiglia

Av Auber

Bd Victor Hugo

R Gast Av Deloye

R Pastorelli

R Blacas

R Verdi

Av Durante

R Alphonse Karr

Pass Émile Négrin

R de l'Hôtel des Postes

R Chauvain

R de la Liberté

25

R Massēna

35

R Paradis

Bd Victor Hugo

R du Maréchal Joffre

20

22

R du Congrès

R Maccarani

Pl
Massēna

R Dalpozzo

R Meyerbeer

24

R de la Buffa

18

Av de Suède

Av de Verdun

Jardin
Albert ler

43

R de France

R Massenet

R Halévy

Bus stop,
200, 400, 500

R St-François de Paule

12

51

Promenade
des Anglais

13

R de Rivoli

1

Promenade des Anglais

14

Q des États-Unis

International
Nice-Côte d'Azur (5.5km);
Cannes (35km)

MEDITERRANEAN
SEA

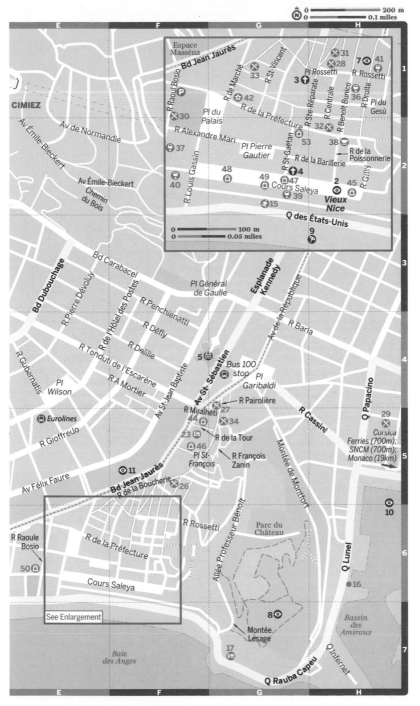

CIMIEZ

Espace Masséna

Bd Jean Jaurès

R Raoul Bosio

R de Marché

R St-Vincent

Pl Rossetti

R Rossetti

R de la Préfecture

R Ste-Réparate

R Centrale

R Benoît Bunico

R Droite

Pl du Gesù

Pl du Palais

R Alexandre Mari

R Louis Gassin

Pl Pierre Gautier

R St-Gaétan

R de la Barillerie

R de la Poissonnerie

R Gilly

Cours Saleya

Vieux Nice

Q des États-Unis

Av Émile-Bieckert

Av de Normandie

Av Émile-Bieckert

Chemin du Bois

0   100 m
0   0.05 miles

0   200 m
0   0.1 miles

Bd Dubouchage

Bd Carabacel

R Pierre Dévoluy

R de l'Hôtel des Postes

R Penchienatti

R Défly

R Tonduti de l'Escarène

R Délille

R A Mortier

Pl Général de Gaulle

Esplanade Kennedy

Av de la République

R Barla

Pl Wilson

Eurolines

R Gioffredo

R Gubernatis

Av St-Jean Baptiste

Av St-Sébastien

Bus 100 stop

Pl Garibaldi

R Pairolière

R Miralhéti

R de la Tour

R François Zanin

Pl St-François

R Cassini

Montée de Montfort

Q Papacino

Corsica Ferries (700m); SNCM (700m); Monaco (19km)

11

Av Félix Faure

Bd Jean Jaurès

R de la Boucherie

R Rossetti

Allée Professeur Bénoît

Parc du Château

Q Lunel

10

R Raoule Bosio

R de la Préfecture

Cours Saleya

See Enlargement

Baie des Anges

Montée Lesage

Bassin des Amiraux

Q Rauba Capeu

Q Internet

93

Nice

⊙ Top Sights

⊙ Sights

🚴 Activities, Courses & Tours

🛏 Sleeping

🍴 Eating

🍷 Drinking & Nightlife

🎭 Entertainment

🛍 Shopping

excellent audioguide is available in English (you will need a form of ID as deposit).

Smartphone users can also download the commentary as an app. It takes about 20 minutes to walk to the museum from the centre (signposted from av de l'Olivetto).

⊙ Central Nice

★ Promenade des Anglais
Architecture

Palm-lined promenade des Anglais, paid for by Nice's English colony in 1822, is a fine stage for a stroll. It's particularly atmospheric in the evening, with Niçois milling about and epic sunsets. Don't miss the magnificent façade of Hôtel Negresco, built in 1912, or art deco Palais de la Méditerranée, saved from demolition in the 1980s and now part of a four-star palace. The promenade follows the whole Baie des Anges (4km) and has a cycle and skating lane.

For a fantastic family outing, rent skates or scooters at Roller Station (www.roller-station. fr; 49 quai des États-Unis; ⊙10am-6pm Nov-Mar, to 7pm Apr-Oct) and whizz along the Prom. You'll need some ID as a deposit. Rentals include protective gear (helmet and pads).

Villa Masséna
Museum

(65 rue de France; ⊙10am-6pm Wed-Mon) FREE The beautiful Musée Masséna, housed in a marvellous Italianate neoclassical villa (1898), retraces Nice and the Riviera's history from the late 18th century to WWII. It's a fascinating journey, with a roll call of monarchs, a succession of nationalities (British, Russians, Americans), the advent of tourism, the prominence of the carnival and more. History is told through a mix of furniture, objects, vintage posters, early photographs,

paintings and the lovely setting (though captions are in French only).

The city of Nice still uses the ground floor rooms for official occasions so it can sometimes close at short notice.

Musée d'Art Moderne et
d'Art Contemporain
Art Museum

(Mamac; www.mamac-nice.org; place Yves Klein; ⊙10am-6pm Tue-Sun) **FREE** European and American avant-garde works from the 1950s to the present are the focus of this museum. Highlights include many works by Nice's New Realists Christo, César, Arman, Yves Klein and Niki de Saint-Phalle. The building's rooftop also works as an exhibition space (with panoramas of Nice to boot).

Promenade du Paillon
Garden

(⊙7am-9pm Oct-Mar, to 11pm Apr-Sep) It's hard to imagine that this beautifully landscaped park was once a bus station, a multistorey car park and an ill-loved square. Completed in October 2013, the park, also known as Coulée Verte, unfolds from the Théâtre National to Place Masséna with a succession of green spaces, play areas and water features and is now a favourite among Niçois for afternoon or evening strolls.

Cathédrale Orthodoxe
Russe St-Nicolas
Cathedral

(www.cathedrale-russe-nice.fr; av Nicolas II; ⊙9am-noon & 2-6pm) Built between 1902 and 1912 to provide a big enough church for the growing Russian community, this cathedral, with its colourful onion domes and rich, ornate interior, is the biggest Russian Orthodox church outside Russia. The cathedral boasts dozens of intricate icons – unfortunately, there is very little in the way of explanation for visitors.

🏃 Activities

Nice's beaches are all pebbly; sensitive behinds should therefore opt for a comfy mattress at one of its 14 private beaches (€15 to €22 per day). Out of the free public sections of beach (with lifeguards, first-aid posts and cold showers), Plage Publique des Ponchettes, opposite Vieux Nice, is the most popular (and don't worry about your bottom, many hotels lend you mats!).

Most beaches also offer a raft of activities, from beach volleyball to jet-skis and pedalos.

The best way to discover Nice's rich heritage is to take a guided walking tour. The tourist office (p100) runs a 2½-hour Vieux Nice tour in English (adult/child €12/6), at 9.30am on Saturday.

Centre du Patrimoine
Walking Tour

(75 quai des Etats-Unis; adult/child €5/free; ⊙8.30am-1pm & 2-5pm Mon-Thu) The Centre du Patrimoine runs thematic two-hour walking tours. English-language tours must be booked two days in advance. The tourist office has a full listing.

Trans Côte d'Azur
Boat Tour

(www.trans-cote-azur.com; quai Lunel; ⊙Apr-Oct) To escape the crowds, take a scenic cruise along the coast. Trans Côte d'Azur runs one-hour trips along the Baie des Anges and the Rade de Villefranche (adult/child €17.5/12) from April to October. From mid-June to mid-September it also runs regular excursions to Île Ste-Marguerite (€38/28, crossing one hour), St-Tropez (€63/48, crossing 2½ hours) and Monaco (€36/27.5, crossing 45 minutes). Reservations are essential.

L'OpenTour
Bus Tour

(www.nice.opentour.com; opposite 109 quai des Etats-Unis, 1-day pass adult/child €22/8) With headphone commentary in several languages, the open-topped bus tours (1½ hours) give you a good overview of Nice. You can hop on or off at any one of 12 stops, including sights in out-of-the-way Cimiez.

⭐ Festivals & Events

Carnaval de Nice
Carnival

(www.nicecarnaval.com; ⊙Feb) Held each year around Mardi Gras (Shrove Tuesday) since 1294 – highlights include the *batailles de fleurs* (battles of flowers), and the ceremonial burning of the carnival king on promenade des Anglais, followed by a fireworks display. People wearing fancy dress can access restricted areas for free.

Nice Jazz Festival
Music Festival

(www.nicejazzfestival.fr; ⊙Jul) France's original jazz festival has taken on a life of its own in its new location off promenade des Anglais; fringe concerts are popping up all around the venue, from Massena and the shopping streets around Rue de France to Vieux Nice. The Nice Jazz Festival itself remains as highbrow as ever.

Celebrating the *batailles de fleurs* (battle of flowers) at Carnaval de Nice (p95)

🛏 Sleeping

Nice has a suite of places to sleep, from stellar backpacker hostels to international art-filled icons. Prices jump during summer and also for regional festivals such as Monaco's Grand Prix.

Hôtel Solara   Hotel €

(📞 04 93 88 09 96; www.hotelsolara.com; 7 rue de France; s/d/tr/q €65/85/120/150; ❄🕿) Were it not for its fantastic location on pedestrian rue de France and the sensational terraces that half the rooms boast, we'd say the Solara was an honest-to-goodness budget-friendly choice with impeccable rooms. But with those perks (and did we mention the small fridges in each room for that evening rosé?), it is a hidden gem.

Villa Saint-Exupéry Beach Hostel   Hostel €

(📞 04 93 16 13 45; www.villahostels.com; 6 rue Sacha Guitry; dm/d €25/70; ❄@🕿) This hostel understands better than anyone what independent travellers need: facilities galore (bar, kitchen, chill-out lounge, free computers, gym, games room etc), friendly multilingual staff, tons of advice on Nice and the Riviera, and budget-friendly prices. The dorms are a bit drab but for the time you'll spend in them...

Hôtel Wilson   Hotel €

(📞 04 93 85 47 79; www.hotel-wilson-nice.com; 39 rue de l'Hôtel des Postes; s/d €55/69; 🕿) Many years of travelling, an experimental nature and exquisite taste have turned Jean-Marie's rambling flat into a compelling place to stay. The 16 rooms have individual, carefully crafted decor, and share the eclectic dining room. The cheapest rooms also share bathrooms.

★ Nice Pebbles   Self-Contained €€

(📞 04 97 20 27 30; www.nicepebbles.com; 1-/3-bedroom apt from €107/220; ❄🕿) Have you ever dreamt of feeling like a real Niçois? Coming back to your designer pad in Vieux Nice, opening a bottle of ice-cold rosé and feasting on market goodies? Nice Pebbles' concept is simple: offering the quality of a four-star boutique hotel in holiday flats. The apartments (one to three bedrooms) are gorgeous and equipped to high standards.

Guests can expect wi-fi, flat-screen TV, DVD players, fully equipped kitchens and linen bedding in most flats, and in some cases, swimming pool, balcony or terrace etc.

Nice Garden Hôtel   Boutique Hotel €€

(📞 04 93 87 35 62; www.nicegardenhotel.com; 11 rue du Congrès; s/d €75/100; ❄🕿) Behind heavy iron gates hides this little gem of a hotel: the nine beautifully appointed rooms, the work of the exquisite Marion, are a subtle blend of old and new and overlook a delightful garden with a glorious orange tree. Amazingly, all this charm and peacefulness is just two blocks from the promenade.

Villa la Tour
Boutique Hotel €€

(📞 04 93 80 08 15; www.villa-la-tour.com; 4 rue de la Tour; d €76-183; ❄️📶) New owners since 2012 have injected a new lease of life into this old-town favourite. Rooms have been redecorated according to painters – we loved the Nikki de St Phalle and Vaco rooms. The diminutive flower-decked roof terrace is now complemented by a street terrace ideal for watching Vieux Nice go by.

Villa Rivoli
Boutique Hotel €€

(📞 04 93 88 80 25; www.villa-rivoli.com; 10 rue de Rivoli; s/d/q from €93/107/225; ❄️📶) Built in 1890, this stately villa feels like your own pied-à-terre in the heart of Nice. A marble staircase leads to spotlessly clean character-rich rooms, some with fabric-covered walls, gilt-edged mirrors and marble mantelpieces.

Hôtel Windsor
Boutique Hotel €€

(📞 04 93 88 59 35; www.hotelwindsornice.com; 11 rue Dalpozzo; d €97-205; ❄️@📶🏊) High-profile artists have decorated more than half the rooms at the Windsor with bold, sometimes unsettling designs. Traditional rooms are more soothing yet still nod to the arts with hand-painted murals.

★ Hôtel La Pérouse
Boutique Hotel €€€

(📞 04 93 62 34 63; www.hotel-la-perouse.com; 11 quai Rauba Capeu; d from €330; ❄️@📶🏊) Built into the rock cliff next to Tour Bellanda, La Pérouse captures the vibe of a genteel villa. Lower-floor rooms face the lemon-tree-shaded courtyard and pool; upper-floor rooms have magnificent vistas of the promenade and sea, many with balconies or terraces to make the best of the panorama. Smart accent colours add flair to the traditional decor.

Nice Excelsior
Design Hotel €€€

(📞 04 93 88 18 05; www.excelsiornice.com; 19 av Durante; d €99-359; ❄️📶) This 1892 building is a belle époque beauty. Inside, the hotel has been entirely refurbished, with the designers finding inspiration in Nice as a popular travel destination: the furniture has been custom-made based on old travel trunks, but with a modern, colourful twist, and rooms are decorated with postcardlike sketches of the city.

✕ Eating

Restaurants in Vieux Nice are a mixed bag of tourist traps and genuine good finds. Follow your instincts, or our recommendations. The Niçois love going out so booking is always recommended, especially for evenings and weekends.

★ La Rossettisserie
French €

(📞 04 93 76 18 80; www.larossettisserie.com; 8 rue Mascoïnat; mains €14.50; 🕐 noon-2pm & 7.30-10pm Mon Sat) The Rossettisserie (a lovely play on word on rotisserie – roast house – and Rossetti, the name of the nearby square) only serves succulent, roast meat – beef, chicken, veal, lamb or pork. It comes with a choice of heavenly homemade mash, ratatouille

---

TOP REGIONAL SPECIALITIES

Nice's eponymous salad (crunchy lettuce, anchovies, olives, green beans and tomatoes in its purest form) has travelled far beyond its original shores. But there is much more to Niçois cuisine than *salade Niçoise*. Here are five local specialities you should try:

Stockfish Dried cod soaked in running water for a few days and then simmered with onions, tomatoes, garlic, olives and potatoes.

Socca A pancake made of chickpea flour and olive oil cooked on a griddle with sneezing quantities of black pepper.

Daube A rich beef stew of wine, onions, carrots, tomatoes and herbs; the sauce is often served with gnocchi or ravioli.

Petits farcis Stuffed vegetables (generally onions, courgette, courgette flowers, tomatoes and aubergines).

Pissaladière A pizzalike base topped with onions, garlic, olives and anchovies.

Our selection of Niçois restaurants will see you right on stockfish and daube; otherwise, make a beeline for Chez René Socca (p98) to try the bite-size snacks.

or sautéed potatoes and a mixed salad. The vaulted dining room in the basement is stunning.

★ Chez Palmyre
French €

(☎ 04 93 85 72 32; 5 rue Droite; menu €17; ⊘ noon-1.30pm & 7-9.30pm Mon-Fri) A new chef has breathed new life into this fabulously atmospheric little restaurant, seemingly unchanged for its long life. The kitchen churns out Niçois standards with a light hand, service is sweet and the price fantastic; book ahead, even for lunch.

Fenocchio
Ice Cream €

(www.fenocchio.fr; 2 place Rossetti; ice cream from €2; ⊘ 9am-midnight Feb-Oct) Dither too long over the 70-plus flavours of ice-cream and sorbet at this unforgettable *glacier* (ice-cream shop) and you'll never make it to the front of the queue. Eschew predictable favourites and indulge in a new taste sensation: black olive, rosemary or lavender.

Le Comptoir du Marché
Modern French €

(☎ 04 93 13 45 01; 8 rue du Marché; mains €13-18; ⊘ noon-2.30pm & 7-10.30pm Tue-Sat) With its vintage kitchen decor and recession-proof prices, it's no wonder the Comptoir does so well. There are five or six daily mains scribbled on a chalkboard. The cuisine is a modern twist on French traditional recipes with lots of offals and staples such as lentil stews, confit rabbit and even *os à moelle* (bone marrow).

La Merenda
Niçois €

(www.lamerenda.net; 4 rue Raoul Bosio; mains €14-18; ⊘ noon-2pm & 7-10pm Mon-Fri) Simple, solid Niçois cuisine by former Michelin-starred chef Dominique Le Stanc draws the crowds to this small bistro (you'll be rubbing back and shoulders with fellow customers). The tiny open kitchen stands proud at the back of the room, and the equally small *menu* is chalked on the board. No credit cards.

Chez René Socca
Niçois €

(2 rue Miralhéti; dishes from €3; ⊘ 9am-9pm Tue-Sun, to 10.30pm Jul & Aug, closed Nov; ☑) Forget about presentation and manners; here, it's all about taste. Grab a portion of *socca* (chickpea-flour pancake) or a plate of *petits farcis* (stuffed vegetables) and head across the street to the bar for a *grand pointu* (glass) of red, white or rosé.

Le Bistrot d'Antoine
Modern French €€

(☎ 04 93 85 29 57; 27 rue de la Préfecture; mains €13-24; ⊘ noon-2pm & 7-11pm Tue-Sat) What's so surprising about this super brasserie is how unfazed it is by its incredible success: it is full every night (booking essential), yet the 'bistro chic' cuisine never wavers, the staff are cool as a cucumber, the atmosphere is reliably jovial and the prices incredibly good value for the area.

Luna Rossa
Italian €€

(☎ 04 93 85 55 66; 3 rue Chauvain; mains €16-28; ⊘ noon-3pm & 7-11pm Tue-Fri, 7-11pm Sat; ☑) Luna Rossa is like your dream Mediterranean dinner come true: fresh pasta, exquisitely cooked seafood, sun-kissed vegetables and divine meats. Wash it down with one of the excellent bottles of red or rosé from the cellar.

L'Escalinada
Niçois €€

(☎ 04 93 62 11 71; www.escalinada.fr; 22 rue Pairolière; menu €26, mains €19-25; ⊘ noon-2.30pm & 7-11pm) This charming restaurant has been one of the best places in town for Niçois cuisine for the last half-century: melt-in-your-mouth homemade gnocchi with tasty daube (Provençal beef stew), grilled prawns with garlic and herbs, Marsala veal stew. The staff are delightful and the welcome *kir* (white wine sweetened with blackcurrant syrup) is on the house. No credit cards.

★ Jan
Modern French €€€

(☎ 04 97 19 32 23; www.restaurantjan.com; 12 rue Lascaris; menu €55, mains €26-32; ⊘ noon-3pm & 7.30-10pm Wed-Fri, 7.30-10pm Tue & Sat) Dining in the elegant aquamarine dining room of this gourmet restaurant is a treat – this is French gastronomy at its best, with regal service by maître d' Philippe Foucault and exquisite food by South African wonder chef Jan Hendrik van der Westhuizen. Antipodean influences are light in the *menu* but more pronounced in the wine list.

🍷 Drinking & Nightlife

Vieux Nice's little streets runneth over with local bars and cafes: from a morning espresso to a lunchtime pastis (the tipple of choice in the south of France), a chilled evening beer or a midnight cocktail, the choice is yours.

Les Distilleries Idéales
Cafe

(www.lesdistilleriesideales.fr; 24 rue de la Préfecture; ⊘ 9am-12.30am) Whether you're after an espresso on your way to the cours Saleya market or an aperitif (complete with cheese and charcuterie platters, €5.60) before trying out one of Nice's fabulous restaurants, Les Distilleries is one of the most atmospheric bars in town. Tables on the small street terrace are ideal for watching the world go by. Happy hour is from 6pm to 8pm.

L'Abat-Jour   Bar

(25 rue Benoît Bunico; ⊙ 6.30pm-2.30am) With its vintage furniture, rotating art exhibitions and alternative music, L'Abat-Jour is all the rage with Nice's young and trendy crowd. The basement has live music or DJ sessions as the night darkens.

Snug & Cellar   Pub

(www.snugandcellar.com; cnr rue Droite & rue Rossetti; ⊙ noon-12.30am) The cellar of this pub hosts live music, quizzes and giant screens for sports events. And when there is nothing special going on, it's just a great place for a drink. The atmosphere is more sophisticated than in Nice's other English or Irish pubs and the staff is charming.

Les Trois Diables   Club

(www.les3diables.com; 2 cours Saleya; ⊙ 5pm-2.15am) This stalwart of the party scene in Nice has ensured its longevity thanks to a good-hearted mix of week-night-friendly events (music quiz on Tuesday, karaoke on Wednesday) and live DJs to spice up the weekend. It's student night on Thursday (bring ID). Happy hour runs to 9pm every night.

Le Six   Gay Bar

(www.le6.fr; 6 rue Raoul Bosio; ⊙ 10pm-5am Tue-Sat) Primped and pretty A-gays crowd shoulder to shoulder at Nice's compact, perennially popular 'mo bar. Le Six keeps a busy event/party schedule: guest DJs, karaoke and shower shows.

Ma Nolan's   Pub

(www.ma-nolans.com; 2 rue St-François de Paule; ⊙ noon-2am Mon-Fri, 11am-2am Sat & Sun; ☎) This Irish pub is big, loud and *the* pub of reference for all foreigners in town. With live music,

Outside diners on cours Saleya (p90)

a pub quiz, big sport events and typical pub food (burgers, fish and chips etc), it's a pretty rowdy place. Happy hour is from 6pm to 8pm.

☆ Entertainment

The tourist office has info on Nice's cultural activities listed in its free publications – *Nice Rendez-vous* (monthly) and *Côte d'Azur en Fêtes* (quarterly, www.cotedazur-en-fetes. com) – or consult the weekly *Semaine des Spectacles* (€1, www.semainedesspectacles. fr), available from newsstands on Wednesday. All are in French.

Chez Wayne's   Live Music

(www.waynes.fr; 15 rue de la Préfecture; ☺10am-2am) Raucous watering hole Chez Wayne's is a typical English pub, that looks like it's been plucked out of London, Bristol or Leeds. It features excellent live bands every night and has the best atmosphere in town. The pub is also sports-mad and shows every rugby, football, Aussie Rules, tennis and cricket game worth watching.

Cinéma Rialto   Cinema

(http://lerialto.cine.allocine.fr; 4 rue de Rivoli) Non-dubbed films, with French subtitles.

🛍 Shopping

Nice is a shopper's paradise: as well as the numerous little boutiques in Vieux Nice, you'll find designers around rue de France and the usual franchises at the enormous Nice Étoile (www.nicetoile.com; av Jean Médecin) shopping mall.

Moulin à Huile d'Olive Alziari   Food

(www.alziari.com.fr; 14 rue St-François de Paule; ☺8.30am-12.30pm & 2-7pm Mon-Sat) Superb olive oil, fresh from the mill on the outskirts of Nice, for €17 per litre; Alziari also produces a dizzying variety of tapenades, fresh olives to nibble (plain, stuffed, marinated etc) and various other snacks.

Cave de la Tour   Wine

(www.cavedelatour.com; 3 rue de la Tour; ☺7am-8pm Tue-Sat) Buy wine from *cavistes* (cellar-people) who know what they're talking about: Cave de la Tour has been run by the same family since 1947.

Pâtisserie LAC   Food

(www.patisseries-lac.com; cnr rue de la Préfecture & rue St-Gaëtan; ☺9.30am-1pm & 2.30-7.30pm Tue-Sun) Plump for divine macaroons and chocolates from chef patissier Pascal Lac at the mouth-watering Pâtisserie LAC.

Henri Auer Confiserie   Food

(www.maison-auer.com; 7 rue St-François de Paule) Sweet teeth will love the crystallised fruit sold at the traditional sweet shop Henri Auer Confiserie; the recipes date back to 1820 and the shop is a sight in its own right.

ℹ Information

There are free wi-fi hotspots on cours Saleya, place Garibaldi and promenade du Paillon.

Hôpital St-Roch (☑04 92 03 33 75; www.chu-nice.fr; 5 rue Pierre Dévoluy; ☺24hr) Emergency service.

Police Station (☑04 92 17 22 22; 1 av Maréchal Foch; ☺24hr) Non-French speakers can call ☑04 92 17 20 31, where translators are on hand.

Tourist Office (☑08 92 70 74 07; www.nicetourisme.com; 5 promenade des Anglais; ☺9am-6pm Mon-Sat) There's also a branch at the train station (av Thiers, open 8am to 7pm Monday to Saturday, 10am to 5pm Sunday).

ℹ Getting There & Away

AIR

Nice-Côte d'Azur Airport (NCE; ☑08 20 42 33 33; www.nice.aeroport.fr; 🛜) is France's second-largest airport and has international flights to Europe, North Africa and even the US, with regular as well as low-cost companies. The airport has two terminals, linked by a free shuttle.

BOAT

Nice is the main port for ferries to Corsica. **SNCM** (www.sncm.fr; quai du Commerce) and **Corsica Ferries** (www.corsicaferries.com; quai du Commerce) are the two main companies.

ℹ Getting Around

Nice is relatively spread out but since the weather is often good and the city beautiful and pedestrian-friendly, walking is the best way to get around. For longer journeys, rent a bicycle from Vélo Bleu.

CAR, MOTORCYCLE & BICYCLE

Major car-rental companies have offices at the train station. The best deals are generally via their websites.

To go native, go for two wheels (and be prepared for hefty safety deposits).

Holiday Bikes (www.holiday-bikes.com; 23 rue de Belgique) Rents out 50cc scooters/125cc motorcycles for €30/55.

Vélo Bleu (☑04 93 72 06 06; www.velobleu.org) A shared-bicycle service with over 100 stations around the city – pick up at one, return at another. One-day/week subscriptions costs €1/5, plus usage: free the first 30 minutes, €1 the next 30, then €2 per hour thereafter. Stations in the most popular parts of town are equipped with special terminals where you can register directly with a credit card; otherwise you'll need a mobile phone. The handy Vélo Bleu app allows you to find your nearest station, gives real-time information about the number of bikes available at each and can also calculate itineraries.

St-Paul de Vence

POP 3593

Once upon a time, St-Paul de Vence was a small medieval village atop a hill looking out to sea. Then came the likes of Chagall and Picasso in the postwar years, followed by showbiz stars such as Yves Montand and Roger Moore, and St-Paul shot to fame. The village is now home to dozens of art galleries as well as the exceptional Fondation Maeght.

The village's tiny cobbled lanes get overwhelmingly crowded in high season – come early or late to beat the rush.

◉ Sights

The Village   Historic Quarter

Strolling the narrow streets is how most visitors pass time in St-Paul. The village has been beautifully preserved and the panoramas from the ramparts are stunning. The main artery, rue Grande, is lined with art galleries. The highest point in the village is occupied by the Église Collégiale; the adjoining Chapelle des Pénitents Blancs was redecorated by Belgian artist Folon.

Many more artists lived or passed through St-Paul de Vence, among them Soutine, Léger, Cocteau, Matisse and Chagall. The latter is buried with his wife Vava in the cemetery at the village's southern end (immediately to the right as you enter). The tourist office runs a series of informative, themed, 90-minute guided tours (adult/child €5/free).

Across from the entrance to the fortified village, the pétanque pitch, where many a star has had a spin, is the hub of village life. The tourist office rents out balls (€2) and can organise pétanque lessons (per person €5).

Fondation Maeght   Art Museum

(www.fondation-maeght.com; 623 chemin des Gardettes; adult/child €15/free; ⊙10am-6pm) The region's finest art museum, Fondation Maeght was created in 1964 by art collectors Aimé and Marguerite Maeght. Its collection of 20th-century works is one of the largest in Europe. It is exhibited on a rotating basis, which, along with the excellent temporary exhibitions, guarantees you'll rarely see the same thing twice. Find the *fondation* 500m downhill from the village.

The building was designed by Josep Lluís Sert and is a masterpiece in itself, integrating the works of the very best: a Giacometti courtyard, Miró sculptures dotted across the terraced gardens, coloured-glass windows by Braque and mosaics by Chagall and Tal-Coat.

St-Paul's tourist office runs guided tours (adult/child €5/free); book ahead.

⌂ Sleeping & Eating

Hostellerie Les Remparts   Hotel €€

(☎04 93 24 10 47; www.hostellerielesremparts.com; 72 Grande Rue; d €65-120; ❄️ 🛜) Right in the heart of the old village, in a medieval building, is this charming family-run hotel. The rooms are spacious and furnished in traditional French style (solid wood furniture and flowery spreads) and those overlooking the valley have fantastic views. The bathrooms are dated but functional.

★ Le Tilleul   Modern French €€

(☎04 93 32 80 36; www.restaurant-letilleul.com; place du Tilleul; menu €25, mains €20-31; ⊙8.30am-10.30pm; 🍴) Considering its location on the *remparts*, it could have easily

TOP TIP: TAKE THE SCENIC ROUTE

Most tourists take the main road to go to Fondation Maeght, but Chemin Ste-Claire is much more inspirational. It was Chagall's route to the village, and along the way you'll pass three chapels, a convent and two Chagall reproductions, placed roughly on the spot where he created the originals.

plumbed the depths of a typical tourist trap; instead, divine and beautifully presented dishes grace your table at Le Tilleul and the all-French wine list includes a generous selection of wine by the glass. Sit under the shade of a big blossoming lime tree.

The restaurant is open all day and serves breakfast and afternoon snacks outside of lunch and dinner.

La Colombe d'Or　　　Traditional French €€€

(☑ 04 93 32 80 02; www.la-colombe-dor.com; place de Gaulle; mains €19-55; ⊘noon-2.30pm & 7.30-10.30pm mid-Dec–Oct; 🐾) A Léger mosaic here, a Picasso painting there: these are just some of the original modern artworks at the Golden Dove, the legendary restaurant where impoverished artists paid for meals with their creations. Dining is beneath fig trees in summer or in the art-filled dining room in winter, and the cuisine is surprisingly uncomplicated (terrines, grilled fish). Book well ahead.

❶ Information

Tourist Office (☑ 04 93 32 86 95; www.saint-pauldevence.com; 2 rue Grande; ⊘10am-6pm) The dynamic tourist office runs a number of themed guided tours that delve into the village's illustrious past. Book ahead; some tours are also available in English.

Vence

POP 19.386

Despite its well-preserved medieval centre, visitors often skip Vieux Vence altogether to head straight to Matisse's other-worldly Chapelle du Rosaire. Yet Vence deserves more than a flying visit.

◉ Sights

★ Chapelle du Rosaire　　　Architecture

(Rosary Chapel; www.vence.fr/the-rosaire-chapel.html; 466 av Henri Matisse; adult/child €6/3; ⊘2-5.30pm Mon, Wed & Sat, 10-11.30am & 2-5.30pm Tue & Thu) An ailing Henri Matisse moved to Vence in 1943, where he fell under the care of his former nurse and model Monique Bourgeois, who had since become a Dominican nun. She persuaded him to design this extraordinary chapel for her community, which Matisse considered his masterpiece. The artist designed everything from the decor to the altar and the priest's vestments.

From the road, all you can see are the blue-and-white ceramic roof tiles and a wrought-iron cross and bell tower. Inside, light floods through the glorious blue, green and yellow stained-glass windows. The colours respectively symbolise water/the sky, plants/life, the sun/God's presence; the back windows display Matisse's famous seaweed motif, those on the side a stylised, geometric leaflike shape.

OLAF PROTZE/GETTY IMAGES ©

Chapelle du Rosaire

A line image of the Virgin Mary and child is painted on white ceramic tiles on the northern interior wall. The western wall is dominated by the bolder Chemin de Croix (Stations of the Cross). St Dominic overlooks the altar. Matisse also designed the chapel's stone altar, candlesticks and cross. The beautiful priests' vestments are displayed in an adjoining hall.

The Vieux Vence · Historic Quarter

Much of the historical centre dates back to the 13th century. The Romanesque cathedral on the eastern side of the square was built in the 11th century on the site of an old Roman temple. It contains Chagall's mosaic of Moses (1979), appropriately watching over the baptismal font.

The daring Fondation Émile Hugues (www.museedevence.com; 2 place du Frêne; adult/child €6/free; ⊙10am-12.30pm & 2-6pm Tue-Sun), with its wonderful 20th-century art exhibitions, inside the imposing Château de Villeneuve, is a nice contrast to Vence's historic quarter.

🛏 Sleeping & Eating

★ Le 2 · B&B €€

(☑04 93 24 42 58; www.le2avence.fr; 2 rue des Portiques; d incl breakfast €105-165; ❇🐕) This 'bed & bistro', as it's tagged itself, is a welcome addition to staid Vence. Nicolas and his family have turned this medieval townhouse into a hip new establishment offering four very modern rooms and a pocket-sized cellar featuring local musicians one night a week. Value and atmosphere guaranteed.

La Litote · Modern French €€

(☑04 93 24 27 82; 5 rue de l'Évêché; menu €23, mains €14-20; ⊙noon-2.30pm & 7-10pm Tue-Sat, noon 2.30pm Sun) In an area where the bar is set very high, chef Stéphane Furlan still manages to surprise and delight diners with a regularly changing *menu* that favours quality rather than quantity. Dine alfresco on a little square at the back of the cathedral, or inside the stone-wall dining room with its open fire.

Antibes & Juan-les-Pins

POP 76,349

With its boat-bedecked port, 16th-century ramparts and narrow cobblestone streets festooned with flowers, lovely Antibes is the quintessential Mediterranean town. Picasso,

Max Ernst and Nicolas de Staël were captivated by Antibes, as was a restless Graham Greene (1904–91) who settled here with his lover, Yvonne Cloetta, from 1966 until the year before his death.

Greater Antibes embraces Cap d'Antibes, an exclusive green cape studded with luxurious mansions, and the modern beach resort of Juan-les-Pins. The latter is known for its 2km-long sandy beach and nightlife, a legacy of the sizzling 1920s when Americans swung into town with their jazz music and oh-so-brief swimsuits.

⊙ Sights & Activities

Vieil Antibes · Historic Quarter

Vieil Antibes is a pleasant mix of food shops, boutiques and restaurants. Mornings are a good time to meander along the little alleyways, when the Marché Provençal (Market; cours Masséna; ⊙7am-1pm Tue-Sun Sep-Jun, daily Jul & Aug) is in full swing. Check out the views from the sea walls, from the urban sprawl of Nice to the snowy peaks of the Alps and nearby Cap d'Antibes.

Musée Picasso · Art Museum

(www.antibes-juanlespins.com; Château Grimaldi, 4 rue des Cordiers; adult/child €6/free; ⊙10am-noon & 2-6pm Tue-Sun) The 14th-century Château Grimaldi served as Picasso's studio from July to December 1946. The museum now houses an excellent collection of his works and fascinating photos of him.

The works from Picasso displayed here are extremely varied – lithographs, paintings, drawings and ceramics – showing how versatile and curious an artist he was. The museum also has a fantastic room dedicated to Nicolas de Staël, another painter who adopted Antibes as his home town.

Fort Carré · Historic Site

(rte du Bord de Mer; guided tour only adult/child €3/free; ⊙10am-6pm Tue-Sun Jul & Aug, to 4.30pm Tue-Sun Sep-Jun) The impregnable 16th-century Fort Carré, enlarged by Vauban in the 17th century, dominates the approach to Antibes from Nice. It served as a border defence post until 1860 when Nice, until then in Italian hands, became French. Regrettably, the tours are rather rushed and the explanations superficial; tours depart half-hourly, some guides speak English.

Cap d'Antibes

Cap d'Antibes' 4.8km of wooded shores are the perfect setting for a walk-swim-walk-swim afternoon. Paths are well marked. The tourist office maps show itineraries.

🌺 Festivals & Events

Jazz à Juan   Music Festival

(www.jazzajuan.com) This major festival, celebrated in Juan-les-Pins in mid-July, has been running for more than 50 years. Every jazz great has performed here. The Off fringe festival is the perfect backup option if you haven't got tickets for the main event.

🛏 Sleeping

Relais International de la Jeunesse   Hostel €

(✆ 04 93 61 34 40; www.clajsud.fr; 272 bd de la Garoupe; dm €20; ☺ Apr-Oct; 🛜) With sea views the envy of neighbouring millionaires, this basic-but-friendly hostel is particularly popular with 'yachties' looking for their next job in Antibes' port. Rates include sheets and breakfast. There is a daily lock-out between 11am and 5pm.

Le Relais du Postillon   Hotel €€

(✆ 04 93 34 20 77; www.relaisdupostillon.com; 8 rue Championnet; d €83-149; ✳🛜) Housed in a 17th-century coach house, the great-value Postillon is in the heart of the old town. The new owners did a huge amount of work in 2013: out went the outdated carpet and bathrooms, in came fresh new bathrooms and boutique decor. The cafe-bar downstairs, with its cosy fireplace, is another charmer.

Hôtel La Jabotte   B&B €€

(✆ 04 93 61 45 89; www.jabotte.com; 13 av Max Maurey; s/d from €110/120; ✳ @ 🛜) A hotel with *chambre d'hôte* (B&B) feel, La Jabotte is just 50m from the sea (and 20 minutes' walk from Vieil Antibes). Its 10 Provençal rooms all look out onto an exquisite patio where breakfast is served from spring to autumn.

🍴 Eating

La Ferme au Foie Gras   Delicatessen €

(www.vente-foie-gras.net; 35 rue Aubernon; sandwiches €4-7; ☺ 8am-6pm Tue-Sun) Now, this is our idea of what a good sandwich should be like: filled with foie gras or smoked duck breast, onion chutney or fig jam, truffle cheese and fresh salad. And many people seem to think the same: a queue snakes down from the tiny counter of La Ferme every lunch time.

Le Broc en Bouche   Modern French €€

(✆ 04 93 34 75 60; 8 rue des Palmiers; mains €21-30; ☺ noon-2pm & 7-10pm Thu-Mon) No two chairs, tables or lights are the same at this lovely bistro: instead, every item has been lovingly sourced from antique shops and car boot sales, giving the place a sophisticated but cosy vintage feel. The charming Flo and Fred have put the same level of care and imagination into their cuisine, artfully preparing Provençal and modern French fare.

🍷 Drinking & Nightlife

★ Balade en Provence   Absinthe Bar

(25 cours Masséna; ☺ 6pm-2am) Flirt with the green fairy at this dedicated absinthe bar in the vaulted basement of an olive oil shop. There is an original 1860 zinc bar, five round tables and all the accessories (four-tapped water fountain, sugar cubes etc).

Pick from 25 absinthe varieties (€6 to €10 per glass) and let the knowledgable staff debunk some of the myths shrouding this much reviled spirit. And don't worry, if you're really not keen, there are plenty of other beverages on offer.

La Siesta Club   Club

(rte du Bord de Mer; cover €20; ☺ 7pm-5am Thu-Sat Jun-Sep) This legendary establishment is famous up and down the coast for its summer beachside nightclub and all-night dancing under the stars.

ℹ Information

Tourist Office (✆ 04 22 10 60 10; www.antibes juanlespins.com; 55 bd Charles Guillaumont; ☺ 9am-noon & 2-6pm Mon-Sat, 10am-1pm Sun)

Menton

POP 29,512

With the opening of the fantastic Musée Jean Cocteau Collection Séverin Wunderman in November 2011, Menton has become a magnet for Cocteau fans the world over.

◉ Sights & Activities

The town's epicentre is pedestrian rue St-Michel, where ice-cream parlours and souvenir shops jostle for space.

★ Musée Jean Cocteau
Collection Séverin Wunderman   Gallery

(www.museecocteaumenton.fr; 2 quai Monléon; combined admission with Musée du Bastion adult/child €8/free; ⊘10am-6pm Wed-Mon) In 2005, art collector Séverin Wunderman donated some 1500 Cocteau works to Menton, on the condition that the town build a dedicated Cocteau museum. And what a museum Menton built: opened in 2011, the futuristic, low-rise building has breathed new life into the slumbering city and provides a wonderful space to make sense of Cocteau's eclectic work. The collection includes drawings, ceramics, paintings and cinematographic work. Explanations are in French, English and Italian throughout.

The admission fee includes the Musée du Bastion, which Cocteau designed.

Musée du Bastion   Art Museum

(quai Napoléon III; combined admission with Musée Jean Cocteau adult/child €8/frcc; ⊘10am-6pm Wed-Mon) Cocteau loved Menton. It was following a stroll along the seaside that he got the idea of turning the disused 17th-century seafront bastion into a monument to his work. He restored the building himself, decorating the alcoves, outer walls and reception hall with pebble mosaics. The works on display change regularly.

Vieille Ville   Historic Quarter

Menton's old town is a cascade of pastel-coloured buildings. Meander the historic quarter all the way to the Cimetière du Vieux Château (montée du Souvenir; ⊘7am-8pm May-Sep, to 6pm Oct-Apr) for great views. From place du Cap a ramp leads to Southern France's grandest baroque church, the Italianate Basilique St-Michel Archange (place de l'Église St-Michel; ⊘3pm-5pm Mon-Fri); its creamy façade is flanked by a 35m-tall clock tower and 53m-tall steeple (1701–03).

Jardin de la Serre
de la Madone   Garden

(www.serredelamadone.com; 74 rte de Gorbio; adult/child €8/free; ⊘10am-6pm Tue-Sun) Beautiful if slightly unkempt, this garden was designed by American botanist Lawrence Johnston. He planted dozens of rare plants picked up from his travels around the world. Abandoned for decades, it has been mostly restored to its former glory. Guided tours take place daily at 3pm. To get here take bus 7 to the 'Serre de la Madone' stop.

⌶ Sleeping & Eating

Accommodation gets booked up months in advance, and prices also soar, for the Fête du Citron in February; plan ahead.

Hôtel Lemon   Hotel €

(⌕04 93 28 63 63; www.hotel-lemon.com; 10 rue Albert 1er; s/d/tr/q €59/69/85/125; ⊛) Housed in a nicely renovated 19th-century villa, Hôtel Lemon has spacious, minimalist rooms in shades of white, and funky bright red or lemon-yellow bathrooms. Wi-fi only works on the ground floor.

★ Hôtel Napoléon   Boutique Hotel €€€

(⌕04 93 35 89 50; www.napoleon-menton.com; 29 porte de France; d €89-345; ⊛@⊛⊛) Standing tall on the seafront, the Napoléon is Menton's most stylish option. Everything from the pool, the restaurant-bar and the back garden (a heaven of freshness in summer) has been beautifully designed. Rooms are decked out in white and blue, with Cocteau drawings on headboards. Sea-facing rooms have balconies but are a little noisier because of the traffic.

The two top-floor suites with seaviews are sensational, with floor-to-ceiling windows, larger balconies and great views from the bath tub!

Sucre & Salés   Cafe €

(8 promenade Maréchal Leclerc; cakes/sandwiches €3/5; ⊘6.30am-8pm; ⊛) Conveniently located opposite the bus station, Sucre & Salés is a contemporary spot to enjoy a coffee, cake or well-stuffed baguette sandwich.

Le Cirke   Seafood €€

(www.restaurantlecirke.com; 1 square Victoria; menu €28, mains €18-35) From paella to bouillabaisse (fish stew), this smart Italian-run restaurant is the place to turn to for delicious seafood. The wine list is a mix of Italian and French references and the service is as sunny as Menton itself.

ⓘ Information

Tourist Office (⌕04 92 41 76 76; www.tourisme-menton.fr; 8 av Boyer; ⊘9am-12.30pm & 2-6pm Mon-Sat)

ROAD TRIP ESSENTIALS

France Driving Guide

With stunning landscapes, superb highways and one of the world's most scenic and comprehensive secondary road networks, France is a road-tripper's dream come true.

DRIVING LICENCE & DOCUMENTS

Drivers must carry the following at all times:

➡ passport or an EU national ID card

➡ valid driving licence (*permis de conduire;* most foreign licences can be used in France for up to a year)

➡ car-ownership papers, known as a *carte grise* (grey card)

➡ proof of third-party liability *assurance* (insurance)

An International Driving Permit (IDP) is not required when renting a car but can be useful in the event of an accident or police stop, as it translates and vouches for the authenticity of your home licence.

Driving Fast Facts

Right or left? Drive on the right

Legal driving age 18

Top speed limit 130km/h on *autoroutes* (highways, motorways)

Signature car Citroën 2CV

INSURANCE

Third-party liability insurance *(assurance au tiers)* is compulsory for all vehicles in France, including cars brought from abroad. Normally, cars registered and insured in other European countries can circulate freely. Contact your insurance company before leaving home to make sure you're covered, and to verify whom to call in case of a breakdown or accident.

In a minor accident with no injuries, the easiest way for drivers to sort things out with their insurance companies is to fill out a *Constat Amiable d'Accident Automobile* (accident report), a standardised way of recording important details about what happened. In rental cars it's usually in the packet of documents in the glove compartment. Make sure the report includes any proof that the accident was not your fault. If it *was* your fault you may be liable for a hefty insurance deductible/excess. Don't sign anything you don't fully understand. If necessary, contact the **police** (☑17).

French-registered cars have their insurance-company details printed on a little green square affixed to the windscreen (windshield).

Road Trip Websites

AUTOMOBILE ASSOCIATIONS

RAC (www.rac.co.uk/driving-abroad/france) Info for British drivers on driving in France.

CONDITIONS & TRAFFIC

Bison Futé (www.bison-fute.equipement.gouv.fr)

Les Sociétés d'Autoroutes (www.autoroutes.fr)

ROUTE MAPPING

Mappy (www.mappy.fr)

Via Michelin (www.viamichelin.com)

Local Expert: Driving Tips

Driving tips for France from Bert Morris, research consultant for IAM (www.iam.org.uk) and former motoring policy director for the AA:

➡ First thing if you're British: watch your instinct to drive on the left. Once I was leaving a supermarket using the left-turn exit lane. I turned by instinct into the left lane of the street and nearly had a head-on collision. My golden rule: when leaving a parking lot, petrol station or motorway off-ramp, do it on the right and your instinct to stay right will kick in.

➡ French law says to give way to traffic on the right, even when you're on a main road. So I advise people to ease off on the foot whenever you get to a junction.

➡ Never go below a third of a tank, even if you think there's cheaper petrol further down the road; sometimes the next station's a long way off. My approach is, don't fret about cost; you're on holiday!

HIRING A CAR

To hire a car in France, you'll need to be older than 21, with an international credit card. Drivers under 25 usually must pay a surcharge.

All car-hire companies provide mandatory third-party liability insurance, but prices and conditions for collision-damage waiver insurance (CDW, or *assurance tous risques*) vary greatly from company to company. Purchasing the CDW can substantially reduce the *franchise* (deductible/excess) that you'll be liable for if the car is damaged or stolen, but car-hire companies sometimes charge exorbitant rates for this protection; if you travel frequently, sites such as www.insurance4carhire.com may provide a cheaper alternative. Your credit card may also cover CDW if you use it to pay for the rental; verify conditions and details with your card issuer.

Arranging your car hire from home is usually considerably cheaper than a walk-in rental, but beware of online offers that don't include CDW or you may be liable for up to 100% of the car's value.

Be sure your car has a spare tyre (it's not uncommon for rentals to be missing these).

International car-hire companies:

Avis (www.avis.com)

Budget (www.budget.com)

Europcar (www.europcar.com)

Hertz (www.hertz.fr)

National-Citer (www.nationalcar.com)

Sixt (www.sixt.com)

French car-hire companies:

ADA (www.ada.fr)

DLM (www.dlm.fr)

France Cars (www.francecars.fr)

Locauto (www.locauto.fr)

Renault Rent (www.renault-rent.com)

Rent a Car Système (www.rentacar.fr)

Internet-based discount brokers:

Auto Europe (www.autoeurope.com)

DriveAway Holidays (driveaway.com.au)

Easycar (www.easycar.com)

Holiday Autos (www.holidayautos.co.uk)

Rental cars with automatic transmission are rare in France; book well ahead for these.

For insurance reasons, rental cars are usually prohibited on ferries, for example to Corsica.

BRINGING YOUR OWN VEHICLE

Any foreign motor vehicle entering France must display a sticker or licence plate identifying its country of registration. Right-hand-drive vehicles brought from the UK or Ireland must have deflectors affixed to the headlights to avoid dazzling oncoming traffic.

MAPS

Michelin's excellent, detailed regional driving maps are highly recommended as a companion to this book, as they will help you navigate back roads and explore alternative routes; IGN's maps are ideal for more specialised activities such as hiking and cycling. Look for both at newsagents, bookshops, airports, supermarkets, tourist offices and service stations along the autoroute.

Institut Géographique National (IGN; www.ign.fr) Publishes regional fold-out maps as well as an all-France volume, *France – Routes, Autoroutes*. Has a great variety of 1:50,000-scale hiking maps, specialised *cyclocartes* (cycling maps) and themed maps showing wine regions, museums etc.

Michelin (boutiquecartesetguides.miche lin.fr) Sells excellent, tear-proof yellow-orange 1:200,000-scale regional maps tailor-made for cross-country driving, with precise coverage of smaller back roads.

ROADS & CONDITIONS

France has one of Europe's densest highway networks. There are four types of intercity roads:

Autoroutes (highway names beginning with A) Multilane divided highways, usually with tolls *(péages)*. Generously outfitted with rest stops.

Routes Nationales (N, RN) National highways. Some sections have divider strips.

Routes Départementales (D) Local highways and roads.

Routes Communales (C, V) Minor rural roads.

The last two categories, while slower, offer some of France's most enjoyable driving experiences.

Road Distances (KM)

	Bayonne	Bordeaux	Brest	Caen	Cahors	Calais	Chambéry	Cherbourg	Clermont-Ferrand	Dijon	Grenoble	Lille	Lyon	Marseille	Nantes	Nice	Paris	Perpignan	Strasbourg	Toulouse
Bordeaux	184																			
Brest	811	623																		
Caen	764	568	376																	
Cahors	307	218	788	661																
Calais	164	876	710	339	875															
Chambéry	860	651	120	800	523	834														
Cherbourg	835	647	399	124	743	461	923													
Clermont-Ferrand	564	358	805	566	269	717	295	689												
Dijon	807	619	867	548	378	572	273	671	279											
Grenoble	827	657	1126	806	501	863	56	929	300	302										
Lille	997	809	725	353	808	112	767	476	650	505	798									
Lyon	831	528	1018	698	439	755	103	820	171	194	110	687								
Marseille	700	651	1271	1010	521	1067	344	1132	477	506	273	999	314							
Nantes	513	326	298	292	491	593	780	317	462	656	787	609	618	975						
Nice	858	810	1429	1168	679	1225	410	1291	636	664	337	1157	473	190	1131					
Paris	771	583	596	232	582	289	565	355	424	313	571	222	462	775	384	932				
Perpignan	499	451	1070	998	320	1149	478	1094	441	640	445	1081	448	319	773	476	857			
Strasbourg	1254	1066	1079	730	847	621	496	853	584	335	551	522	488	803	867	804	490	935		
Toulouse	300	247	866	865	116	991	565	890	890	727	533	923	536	407	568	564	699	205	1022	
Tours	536	348	490	246	413	531	611	369	369	418	618	463	449	795	197	952	238	795	721	593

Motorcyclists will find France great for touring, with high-quality roads and stunning scenery. Just make sure your wet-weather gear is up to scratch.

Note that high mountain passes, especially in the Alps, may be closed from as early as September to as late as June. Conditions are posted at the foot of each pass ('*ouvert*' on a green background means open, '*ferme*' on a red background means closed). Snow chains or studded tyres are required in wintry weather.

ROAD RULES

Enforcement of French traffic laws has been stepped up considerably in recent years. Speed cameras are increasingly common, as are radar traps and unmarked police vehicles. Fines for many infractions are given on the spot.

Speed Limits

Speed limits outside built-up areas (unless signposted otherwise):

Undivided N and D highways 90km/h (80km/h when raining)

Non-autoroute divided highways 110km/h (100km/h when raining)

Autoroutes 130km/h (110km/h when raining)

Unless otherwise signposted, a limit of 50km/h applies in *all* areas designated as built up, no matter how rural they may appear. You must slow to 50km/h the moment you come to a town entry sign; this speed limit applies until you pass a town exit sign with a diagonal bar through it.

You're expected to already know the speed limit for various types of roads; that's why most speed-limit signs begin with the word *rappel* (reminder). You can be fined for going as little as 10km over the speed limit.

Alcohol

➡ The blood-alcohol limit is 0.05% (0.5g per litre of blood) – the equivalent of two glasses of wine for a 75kg adult.

➡ Police often conduct random breathalyser tests. Penalties can be severe, including imprisonment.

Motorcycles

➡ Riders of any two-wheeled motorised vehicle must wear a helmet.

➡ No special licence is required to ride a motorbike with an engine smaller than 50cc, which is why rental scooters are often rated at 49.9cc.

➡ As of 1 January 2013, all riders of motorcycles 125cc or larger must wear high-visibility reflective clothing measuring at least 150 sq cm on their upper bodies.

Child Seats

➡ Up to age 10 (or 1.4m tall), children must use a size-appropriate child seat or booster.

➡ Children under 10 cannot ride in the front seat (unless the back is already occupied by other children under 10).

➡ A child under 13kg must travel in a backward-facing child seat.

Priority to the Right

Under the *priorité à droite* (priority to the right) rule, any car entering an intersection from a road on your right has the right of way. Don't be surprised if locals courteously cede the right of way when you're about to turn from an alley onto a highway, yet boldly assert their rights when you're the one zipping down a main road.

Priorité à droite is suspended on some main roads marked with a yellow diamond-shaped sign. The same sign with a diagonal bar through it reinstates the *priorité à droite* rule.

At roundabouts where you don't have the right of way (ie the cars already in the roundabout do), you'll see signs reading *vous n'avez pas la priorité* (you do not have right of way) or *cédez le passage* (yield/give way).

Driving Problem-Buster

I can't speak French; will that be a problem? While it's preferable to learn some French before travelling, French road signs are mostly of the 'international symbol' variety, and English is increasingly spoken among the younger generation. Our Language chapter can help you navigate some common roadside emergency situations; in a worst-case scenario, a good attitude and sign language can go a long way.

What should I do if my car breaks down? Safety first: turn on your flashers, put on a safety vest (legally required, and provided in rental-car glove compartments) and place a reflective triangle (also legally required) 30m to 100m behind your car to warn approaching motorists. Call for **emergency assistance** (☏112) or walk to the nearest orange roadside call box (placed every 2km along French *autoroutes*). If renting a vehicle, your car-hire company's service number may help expedite matters. If travelling in your own car, verify before leaving home whether your local auto club has reciprocal roadside-assistance arrangements in France.

What if I have an accident? For minor accidents you'll need to fill out a *constat amiable d'accident* (accident statement, typically provided in rental-car glove compartments) and report the accident to your insurance and/or rental-car company. If necessary, contact the **police** (☏17).

What should I do if I get stopped by the police? Show your passport (or EU national ID card), licence and proof of insurance. See our Language chapter for some handy phrases.

What's the speed limit in France and how is it enforced? Speed limits (indicated by a black-on-white number inside a red circle) range from 30km/h in small towns to 130km/h on the fastest *autoroutes*. If the motorbike police pull you over, they'll fine you on the spot or direct you to the nearest *gendarmerie* (police station) to pay. If you're caught by a speed camera (placed at random intervals along French highways), the ticket will be sent to your rental-car agency, which will bill your credit card, or to your home address if you're driving your own vehicle. Fines depend on how much you're over the limit.

How do French tolls work? Many French *autoroutes* charge tolls. Take a ticket from the machine upon entering the highway and pay as you exit. Some exit booths are staffed by people; others are automated and will accept only chip-and-PIN credit cards or coins.

What if I can't find anywhere to stay? During summer and holiday periods, book accommodation in advance whenever possible. Local tourist offices can sometimes help find you a bed during normal business hours. Otherwise, try your luck at national chain hotels such as Etap and Formule 1 (p116), which are typically clustered at *autoroute* exits outside urban areas.

Other Rules

➡ All passengers, including those in the back seat, must wear seat belts.

➡ Mobile phones may be used only if equipped with a hands-free kit or speakerphone.

➡ Turning right on a red light is illegal.

➡ All vehicles driven in France must carry a high-visibility safety vest, a reflective triangle, a spare set of headlight bulbs and (as of 1 July 2012) a portable, single-use breathalyser kit. Noncompliant drivers are subject to fines.

For pictures and descriptions of common French road signs, see the inside back cover.

France Playlist

Bonjour Rachid Taha and Gaetan Roussel

Coeur Vagabond Gus Viseur

La Vie en Rose Édith Piaf

Minor Swing Django Reinhardt

L'Americano Akhenaton

Flower Duet from Lakmé Léo Delibes

De Bonnes Raisons Alex Beaupain

PARKING

In city centres, most on-the-street parking places are *payant* (metered) from 9am to 7pm Monday to Saturday (sometimes with a midday break). Buy a ticket at the nearest *horodateur* (coin-fed ticket machine) and place it on your dashboard with the time stamp clearly visible. Bigger cities also have public parking garages.

FUEL

➡ Diesel (*gazole* or *gasoil*) – €1.35/L; many cars in France run on diesel.

➡ *Essence* (gas/petrol), or *carburant* (fuel) – €1.50/L for 95 unleaded (SP95).

➡ Filling up *(faire le plein)* is most expensive at *autoroute* rest stops, cheapest at hypermarkets.

➡ When renting a car, ask whether it runs on *gazole* or *essence*.

➡ At the pump, diesel nozzles are generally yellow, unleaded petrol (gas) nozzles green.

➡ Many petrol stations close on Sunday afternoon; even in cities, staffed stations are rarely open late.

➡ After-hours purchases (eg at hypermarkets' fully automatic 24-hour stations) can only be made with a credit card that has an embedded PIN chip. If you don't have a chip-and-PIN card, try to get one from your card company before leaving home; chip-and-PIN cards are also required at many toll booths and train-ticket dispensers throughout France.

SATELLITE NAVIGATION SYSTEMS

Sat-nav devices can be helpful in navigating your way around France. They're commonly available at car-rental agencies, or you can bring your own from home. Accuracy is more dependable on main highways than in small villages or on back roads; in rural areas, don't hesitate to fall back on common sense, road signs and a good Michelin map if your sat nav seems to be leading you astray.

SAFETY

Never leave anything valuable inside your car, even in the boot (trunk). Note that thieves can easily identify rental cars, as they have a distinctive number on the licence plate.

Theft is especially prevalent in the south. In cities such as Marseille and Nice, occasional aggressive theft from cars stopped at red lights is also an issue.

RADIO

For news, tune in to the French-language France Info (105.5MHz), the multilanguage RFI (738kHz or 89MHz in Paris) or, in northern France, the BBC World Service (648kHz) and BBC Radio 4 (198kHz). Popular national FM music stations include **NRJ** (www.nrj.fr), **Skyrock** (www.skyrock.fm) and **Nostalgie** (www.nostalgie.fr).

In many areas, Autoroute Info (107.7MHz) has round-the-clock traffic information.

France
Travel Guide

GETTING THERE & AWAY

AIR

International Airports

Rental cars are available at all international airports listed here.

Paris Charles de Gaulle (CDG; www.aeroportsdeparis.fr)

Paris Orly (ORY; www.aeroportsdeparis.fr)

Aéroport de Bordeaux (www.bordeaux.aeroport.fr)

Aéroport de Lille (www.lille.aeroport.fr)

Aéroport Lyon-Saint Exupéry (www.lyonaeroports.com)

EuroAirport (Basel-Mulhouse-Freiburg; www.euroairport.com)

Aéroport Nantes Atlantique (www.nantes.aeroport.fr)

Aéroport Nice Côte d'Azur (societe.nice.aeroport.fr)

Aéroport International Strasbourg (www.strasbourg.aeroport.fr)

Aéroport Toulouse-Blagnac (www.toulouse.aeroport.fr)

CAR & MOTORCYCLE

Entering France from other parts of the EU is usually a breeze – no border checkpoints and no customs – thanks to the Schengen Agreement, signed by all of France's neighbours except the UK, the Channel Islands and Andorra. For these three, old-fashioned document and customs checks are still the norm when exiting France (as well as when entering from Andorra).

Channel Tunnel

The Channel Tunnel (Chunnel), inaugurated in 1994, is the first dry-land link between England and France since the last ice age.

High-speed **Eurotunnel Le Shuttle** (www.eurotunnel.com) trains whisk cars and motorcycles in 35 minutes from Folkestone through the Chunnel to Coquelles, 5km southwest of Calais. Shuttles run 24 hours, with up to three departures an hour during peak time. LPG and CNG tanks are not permitted; gas-powered cars and many campers and caravans have to travel by ferry.

Eurotunnel sets its fares the way budget airlines do: the earlier you book and the lower the demand for a particular crossing, the less you pay; same-day fares can cost a small fortune. Fares for a car, including up to nine passengers, start at £30.

SEA

P&O Ferries (www.poferries.com) and **DFDS Seaways** (www.dfdsseaways.co.uk) both operate regular trans-Channel car ferry service from England to France (primarily from Dover to Calais, with less frequent services from Dover to Dunkirk). **Brittany Ferries** (www.brittanyferries.com) offers additional services from Plymouth, Portsmouth and Poole to the French ports of Roscoff, St-Malo, Cherbourg and Caen.

Ferry companies typically offer discounts for advance booking and/or off-peak travel. Seasonal demand is a crucial factor (Christmas, Easter, UK and French school holidays, July and August are especially busy), as is the time of day (an early-evening ferry can cost much more than one at 4am).

For the best fares, check **Ferry Savers** (www.ferrysavers.com).

TRAIN

Rail services link France with virtually every country in Europe. The **Eurostar** (www.eurostar.com) whisks passengers from London to Paris in 2¼ hours.

You can book tickets and get train information from **Rail Europe** (www.raileurope.com). In France ticketing is handled by the national railway company **SNCF** (www.sncf.com). High-speed train travel between France and the UK, Belgium, the Netherlands, Germany and Austria is covered by **Railteam** (www.railteam.co.uk) and **TGV-Europe** (www.tgv-europe.com).

Avis (www.avis.fr), in partnership with **SNCF** (www.voyages-sncf.com/train/train-avis), has rental-car agencies in most major French railway stations. Cars booked through the SNCF website may be picked up from an SNCF representative after hours if the Avis office is closed.

DIRECTORY A–Z

ACCOMMODATION

Be it a fairy-tale château, a boutique hideaway or floating pod on a lake, France has accommodation to suit every taste, mood and pocket.

Categories

Budget covers everything from hostels to small, simple family-run places; midrange means a few extra creature comforts such as satellite TV and free wi-fi; and top-end places stretch from luxury five-star palaces with air conditioning, pools and restaurants to boutique-chic chalets in the Alps.

Costs

Accommodation costs vary wildly between seasons and regions: what will buy you a night in a romantic *chambre d'hôte* (B&B) in the countryside may only get you a dorm bed in a major city or high-profile ski resort.

Reservations

Midrange, top-end and many budget hotels require a credit card to secure a reservation. Tourist offices can often advise on availability and reserve for you, sometimes charging a small fee.

Seasons

➡ In ski resorts, high season is Christmas, New Year and the February–March school holidays.

➡ On the coast, high season is summer, particularly August.

➡ Hotels in inland cities often charge low-season rates in summer.

➡ Rates often drop outside the high season – in some cases by as much as 50%.

➡ In business-oriented hotels in cities, rooms are most expensive from Monday to Thursday and cheaper over the weekend.

➡ In the Alps, hotels usually close between seasons, from around May to mid-June and from mid-September to early December; many addresses in Corsica only open April to October.

B&Bs

For charm, it's hard to beat privately run *chambres d'hôte* (B&Bs), available throughout rural France. By law a *chambre d'hôte must* have no more than five rooms and breakfast must be included in the price; some hosts prepare home-cooked evening meals *(table d'hôte)* for an extra charge of €20 to €30. Pick up lists of *chambres d'hôte* at local tourist offices, or consult the following websites:

Bienvenue à la Ferme (www.bienvenue-a-la-ferme.com) Farmstays.

Chambres d'hôtes de Charme (www.guidesdecharme.com) Boutique B&Bs.

Chambres d'Hôtes France (www.chambresdhotesfrance.com)

en France (www.bbfrance.com) B&Bs and *gîtes* (self-catering cottages).

Fleurs de Soleil (www.fleursdesoleil.fr) Stylish *maisons d'hôte,* mainly in rural France.

Gîtes de France (www.gites-de-france.com) France's primary umbrella organisation for B&Bs and *gîtes*. Search for properties by region,

Practicalities

Time France uses the 24-hour clock and is on Central European Time, which is one hour ahead of GMT/UTC. During daylight-saving time, from the last Sunday in March to the last Sunday in October, France is two hours ahead of GMT/UTC.

TV & DVD TV is Secam; DVDs are zone 2; videos work on the PAL system.

Weights & Measures France uses the metric system.

Sleeping Price Ranges

The following price ranges refer to a double room with private bathroom in high season (breakfast is not included, except at B&Bs).

€	less than €80
€€	€80–180
€€€	more than €180

theme (with kids, by the sea, gourmet, etc), activity (fishing, wine tasting etc) or facilities (pool, dishwasher, fireplace, baby equipment etc).

Guides de Charme (www.guidesdecharme. com) Upmarket B&Bs.

Samedi Midi Éditions (www.samedimidi. com) *Chambres d'hôte* organised by location or theme.

Camping

Camping is extremely popular in France. There are thousands of well-equipped campgrounds, many considerately placed by rivers, lakes and the sea. Gîtes de France and Bienvenue à la Ferme coordinate camping on farms.

➡ Most campgrounds open March or April to late September or October; popular spots fill up fast in summer, when it's wise to book ahead.

➡ Economisers should look out for local, good-value but no-frills *campings municipaux* (municipal campgrounds).

➡ Many campgrounds rent mobile homes with mod cons like heating, kitchen and TV.

➡ Camping 'wild' in nondesignated spots (*camping sauvage*) is illegal in France.

➡ Campsite offices often close during the day.

Websites with campsite listings searchable by location, theme and facilities:

Camping en France (www.camping.fr)

Camping France (www.campingfrance.com)

Guide du Camping (www.guideducamping.com)

HPA Guide (http://camping.hpaguide.com)

Hostels

Hostels in France range from spartan rooms to hip hang-outs with perks aplenty.

➡ In university towns, *foyers d'étudiant* (student dormitories) are sometimes converted for use by travellers during summer.

➡ A dorm bed in an *auberge de jeunesse* (youth hostel) costs from €10.50 to €28 depending on location, amenities and facilities; sheets are always included, breakfast more often than not.

➡ Hostels by the sea or in the mountains sometimes offer seasonal outdoor activities.

➡ French hostels are 100% nonsmoking.

Hotels

We have tried to feature well-situated, independent hotels that offer good value, a warm welcome, at least a bit of charm and a palpable sense of place.

➡ Hotels in France are rated with one to five stars, although the ratings are based on highly objective criteria (eg the size of the entry hall), not the quality of the service, the decor or cleanliness.

➡ French hotels rarely include breakfast in their rates. Unless specified otherwise, prices quoted don't include breakfast, which costs around €7/10/20 in a budget/midrange/top-end hotel.

➡ A double room generally has one double bed (sometimes two singles pushed together!); a room with twin beds (*deux lits*) is usually more expensive, as is a room with a bathtub instead of a shower.

➡ Feather pillows are practically nonexistent in France, even in top-end hotels.

➡ All hotel restaurant terraces allow smoking; if you are sensitive to smoke sit inside or carry a respirator.

Chain Hotels

Chain hotels stretch from nondescript establishments near the *autoroute* (motorway, highway) to central four-star hotels with character. Most conform to certain standards of decor, service and facilities (air-conditioning, free wi-fi, 24-hour check-in etc), and offer competitive rates as well as last-minute, weekend and/or online deals.

Book Your Stay Online

For more accommodation reviews by Lonely Planet authors, check out http://hotels.lonelyplanet.com. You'll find independent reviews, as well as recommendations on the best places to stay. Best of all, you can book online.

Countrywide biggies:

B&B Hôtels (www.hotel-bb.com) Cheap motel-style digs.

Best Western (www.bestwestern.com) Independent two- to four-star hotels, each with its own local character.

Campanile (www.campanile.com) Good-value hotels geared up for families.

Citôtel (www.citotel.com) Independent two- and three-star hotels.

Contact Hôtel (www.contact-hotel.com) Inexpensive two- and three-star hotels.

Etap (www.etaphotel.com) Ubiquitous chain.

Formule 1 (www.hotelformule1.com) Non-descript roadside cheapie.

Ibis (www.ibishotel.com) Midrange pick.

Inter-Hotel (www.inter-hotel.fr) Two- and three-star hotels, some quite charming.

Kyriad (www.kyriad.com) Comfortable midrange choices.

Novotel (www.novotel.com) Family-friendly.

Première Classe (www.premiereclasse.com) Motel-style accommodation.

Sofitel (www.sofitel.com) Range of top-end hotels in major French cities.

ELECTRICITY

European two-pin plugs are standard. France has 230V at 50Hz AC (you may need a transformer for 110V electrical appliances).

230V/50Hz

FOOD

Food-happy France has a seemingly endless variety of eateries; categories listed here are found throughout the country: The Eating & Sleeping sections of this guide include phone numbers for places that require reservations (typically higher-end bistros or family-run enterprises such as *tables d'hôte*).

Auberge Country inn serving traditional fare, often attached to a B&B or small hotel.

Ferme auberge Working farm that cooks up meals – only dinner usually – from local farm products.

Bistro (also spelt *bistrot*) Anything from a pub or bar with snacks and light meals to a small, fully fledged restaurant.

Brasserie Much like a cafe except it serves full meals, drinks and coffee from morning until 11pm or later. Typical fare includes *choucroute* (sauerkraut) and *moules frites* (mussels and fries).

Restaurant Born in Paris in the 18th century, restaurants today serve lunch and dinner five or six days a week.

Cafe Basic light snacks as well as drinks.

Crêperie (also *galetterie*) Casual address specialising in sweet crêpes and savoury *galettes* (buckwheat crêpes).

Salon de Thé Trendy tearoom often serving light lunches (quiche, salads, cakes, tarts, pies and pastries) as well as black and herbal teas.

Table d'hôte (literally 'host's table') Some of the most charming B&Bs serve *table d'hôte* too, a delicious homemade meal of set courses with little or no choice.

Eating Price Ranges

The following price ranges refer to a two-course set menu (ie entrée plus main course or main course plus dessert), with tax and service charge included in the price.

€	less than €20
€€	€20–40
€€€	more than €40

GAY & LESBIAN TRAVELLERS

The rainbow flag flies high in France, a country that left its closet long before many of its European neighbours. *Laissez-faire* perfectly sums up France's liberal attitude towards homosexuality and people's private lives in general. Paris, Bordeaux, Lille, Lyon, Montpellier and Toulouse are among the many cities with thriving gay and lesbian scenes. Attitudes towards homosexuality tend to be more conservative in the countryside and villages. France's lesbian scene is less public than its gay male counterpart.

Publications

Damron (www.damron.com) Publishes English-language travel guides, including the *Damron Women's Traveller* for lesbians and the *Damron Men's Travel Guide* for gays.

Spartacus International Gay Guide (www.spartacusworld.com) A male-only guide with more than 70 pages devoted to France, almost half of which cover Paris. iPhone app too.

Websites

France Queer Resources Directory (www.france.qrd.org) Gay and lesbian directory.

French Government Tourist Office (www.us.franceguide.com/special-interests/gay-friendly) Information about 'the gay-friendly destination par excellence'.

Gay France (www.gay-france.net) Insider tips on gay life in France.

Gayscape (www.gayscape.com) Hundreds of links to gay- and lesbian-related sites.

Gayvox (www.gayvox.com/guide3) Online travel guide to France, with listings by region.

Tasse de Thé (www.tassedethe.com) A *webzine lesbien* with lots of useful links.

INTERNET ACCESS

➡ Wireless (wi-fi) access points can be found at major airports, in many hotels and at some cafes.

➡ Some tourist offices and numerous cafes and bars tout wi-fi hot spots that let laptop owners hook up for free.

➡ To search for free wi-fi hot spots in France, visit www.hotspot-locations.co.uk or www.free-hotspot.com.

➡ Internet cafes are becoming less rife, but at least one can still be found in most large towns and cities. Prices range from €2 to €6 per hour.

➡ If accessing dial-up ISPs with your laptop, you'll need a telephone-plug adaptor, available at large supermarkets.

MONEY

ATMs

Known as *distributeurs automatiques de billets* (DAB) or *points d'argent* in French, ATMs are the cheapest and most convenient way to get money. Those connected to international networks are ubiquitous and usually offer an excellent exchange rate.

Cash

You always get a better exchange rate in-country, but if arriving in France by air or late at night, you may want to bring enough euros to take a taxi to a hotel.

Credit & Debit Cards

➡ Credit and debit cards, accepted almost everywhere in France, are convenient and relatively secure and usually offer a better exchange rate than travellers cheques or cash exchanges.

➡ Credit cards issued in France have embedded chips – you have to type in a PIN to make a purchase.

➡ Visa, MasterCard and Amex can be used in shops and supermarkets and for train travel, car hire and motorway tolls, though some places (eg 24-hour petrol stations, some autoroute toll machines) only take French-style credit cards with chips and PINs.

➡ Don't assume that you can pay for a meal or a budget hotel with a credit card – enquire first.

➡ Cash advances are a supremely convenient way to stay stocked up with euros, but getting cash with a credit card involves both fees (sometimes US$10 or more) and interest – ask your credit-card issuer for details. Debit-card fees are usually much less.

Moneychangers

➡ In Paris and major cities, *bureaux de change* (exchange bureaus) are open longer hours, give faster and easier service and often have better rates than banks.

➡ Some post-office branches exchange travellers cheques and banknotes; most won't take US$100 bills.

Tipping Guide

By law, restaurant and bar prices are *service compris* (include a 15% service charge), so there is no need to leave a *pourboire* (tip). If you were extremely satisfied with the service, however, you can – as many locals do – leave a small 'extra' tip for your waiter or waitress.

bars	round to nearest euro
hotel cleaning staff	€1-1.50 per day
hotel porters	€1-1.50 per bag
restaurants	5-10%
taxis	10-15%
toilet attendants	€0.20-0.50
tour guides	€1-2 per person

OPENING HOURS

Below are standard hours for various types of business in France (note that these can fluctuate by an hour either way in some cases). For individual business listings in this book, we've only included opening hours where they differ significantly from these standards:

banks	9am-noon & 2-5pm Mon-Fri or Tue-Sat
bars	7pm-1am Mon-Sat
cafes	7am or 8am-10pm or 11pm Mon-Sat
nightclubs	10pm-3am, 4am or 5am Thu-Sat
post offices	8.30am or 9am-5pm or 6pm Mon-Fri, 8am-noon Sat
restaurants	lunch noon-2.30pm, dinner 7-11pm six days a week
shops	9am or 10am-7pm Mon-Sat (often with lunch break noon-1.30pm)
supermarkets	8.30am-7pm Mon-Sat, 8.30am-12.30pm Sun

PUBLIC HOLIDAYS

The following *jours fériés* (public holidays) are observed in France:

New Year's Day (Jour de l'An) 1 January.

Easter Sunday and Monday (Pâques and lundi de Pâques) Late March/April.

May Day (Fête du Travail) 1 May.

Victoire 1945 8 May – commemorates the Allied victory in Europe that ended WWII.

Ascension Thursday (Ascension) May – celebrated on the 40th day after Easter.

Pentecost/Whit Sunday and Whit Monday (Pentecôte and lundi de Pentecôte) Mid-May to mid-June – celebrated on the seventh Sunday after Easter.

Bastille Day/National Day (Fête Nationale) 14 July – *the* national holiday.

Assumption Day (Assomption) 15 August.

All Saints' Day (Toussaint) 1 November.

Remembrance Day (L'onze novembre) 11 November – marks the WWI armistice.

Christmas (Noël) 25 December.

SAFE TRAVEL

France is generally a safe place to travel, though crime has risen substantially in recent years. Property crime is much more common than physical violence; it's extremely unlikely that you will be assaulted while walking down the street. Always check your government's travel advisory warnings.

Hunting is traditional and commonplace throughout rural France, and the season runs from September to February. If you see signs reading 'chasseurs' or 'chasse gardée' strung up or tacked to trees, think twice about wandering into the area.

Natural Dangers

➡ There are powerful tides and strong undertows at many places along the Atlantic coast, from the Spanish border north to Brittany and Normandy.

➡ Only swim in zones de baignade surveillée (beaches monitored by life guards).

➡ Be aware of tide times and the high-tide mark if walking on a beach.

➡ Thunderstorms in the mountains and the hot southern plains can be extremely sudden and violent.

➡ Check the weather report before setting out on a long walk and be prepared for sudden temperature drops if you're heading into the high country of the Alps or Pyrenees.

➡ Avalanches pose a significant danger in the Alps.

Theft

There's no need to travel in fear, but it is worth taking a few simple precautions against theft.

➡ Break-ins to parked cars are not uncommon. Never leave anything valuable inside your car, even in the boot (trunk).

➡ Aggressive theft from cars stopped at red lights is occasionally a problem, especially in Marseille and Nice. As a precaution, lock your car doors and roll up the windows in major urban areas.

➡ Pickpocketing and bag snatching (eg in dense crowds and public places) are prevalent in big cities, particularly Paris. Be especially vigilant for bag-snatchers at outdoor cafes and beaches.

– – – – – – – – – – – – – – – – –
TELEPHONE
Mobile Phones

➡ French mobile-phone numbers begin with 📱06 or 📱07.

➡ France uses GSM 900/1800, which is compatible with the rest of Europe and Australia but not with the North American GSM 1900 or the totally different system in Japan (though some North Americans have tri-band phones that work in France).

➡ Check with your service provider about roaming charges – dialling a mobile phone from a fixed-line phone or another mobile can be incredibly expensive.

➡ It may be cheaper to buy your own French SIM card – and locals you meet are much more likely to ring you if your number is French.

➡ If you already have a compatible phone, you can slip in a SIM card (€20 to €30) and rev it up with prepaid credit, though this is likely to run out fast as domestic prepaid calls cost about €0.50 per minute.

➡ Recharge cards are sold at most tabacs and newsagents.

➡ SIMs are available at the ubiquitous outlets run by France's three mobile-phone companies, **Bouygues** (www.bouyguestelecom.fr), **Orange** (www.orange.com) and **SFR** (www. sfr.com).

Phone Codes

Calling France from abroad Dial your country's international access code, then 📱33 (France's country code), then the 10-digit local number *without* the initial zero.

Calling internationally from France Dial 📱00 (the international access code), the *indicatif* (country code), the area code (without the initial zero if there is one) and the local number. Some country codes are posted in public telephones.

Directory enquiries For national *service des renseignements* (directory enquiries) dial 📱11 87 12 (€1.46 per call, plus €0.45 per minute), or use the service for free online at www.118712.fr.

Emergency numbers Can be dialled from public phones without a phonecard.

Hotel calls Hotels, *gîtes,* hostels and *chambres d'hôte* are free to meter their calls as they like. The surcharge is usually around €0.30 per minute but can be higher.

International directory enquiries For numbers outside France, dial 📱11 87 00 (€2 to €3 per call).

Phonecards

➡ For explanations in English and other languages on how to use a public telephone, push the button engraved with a two-flags icon.

➡ For both international and domestic calling, most public phones operate using either a credit card or two kinds of *télécartes* (phonecards): *cartes à puce* (cards with a magnetic chip) issued by Orange (formerly France Télécom) and sold at post offices for €8 or €15; and *cartes à code* (cards where you dial a free access number and then the card's scratch-off code), sold at *tabacs*, newsagents and post offices.

➡ Phonecards with codes offer *much* better international rates than Orange chip cards or Country Direct services (for which you are billed at home by your long-distance carrier).

➡ The shop you buy a phonecard from should be able to tell you which type is best for the country you want to call. Using phonecards from a home phone is much cheaper that using them from public phones or mobile phones.

TOILETS

Public toilets around France are signposted WC or *toilettes*. These range from spiffy 24-hour mechanical self-cleaning toilets costing around €0.50 to hole-in-the-floor *toilettes à la turque* (squat toilets) at older establishments and motorway stops. In the most basic places you may need to supply your own paper.

The French are more blasé about unisex toilets than elsewhere, so save your blushes when tiptoeing past the urinals to reach the ladies' loo.

TOURIST INFORMATION

Almost every city, town, village and hamlet has a clearly signposted *office de tourisme* (government-run tourist office) or *syndicat d'initiative* (tourist office run by local merchants). Both can supply you with local maps as well as details on accommodation, restaurants and activities such as walking, cycling or wine tasting. Useful websites:

French Government Tourist Office (www.franceguide.com) The low-down on sights, activities, transport and special-interest holidays in all of France's regions. Brochures can be downloaded online. There are links to country-specific websites.

Réseau National des Destinations Départementales (www.fncdt.net) Listing of CRT (regional tourist board) websites.

TRAVELLERS WITH DISABILITIES

While France presents evident challenges for *handicapés* (people with disabilities) – namely cobblestone, cafe-lined streets that are a nightmare to navigate in a wheelchair, a lack of curb ramps, older public facilities and many budget hotels without lifts – you can still enjoy travelling here with a little careful planning.

Whether you are looking for wheelchair-friendly accommodation, sights, attractions or restaurants, these associations and agencies can help:

Association des Paralysés de France (APF; www.apf.asso.fr) National organisation for people with disabilities, with offices throughout France.

Tourisme et Handicaps (www.tourisme-handicaps.org) Issues the 'Tourisme et Handicap' label to tourist sites, restaurants and hotels that comply with strict accessibility and usability standards. Different symbols indicate the sort of access afforded to people with physical, mental, hearing and/or visual disabilities.

VISAS

For up-to-date details on visa requirements, see the website of the **Ministère des Affaires Étrangères** (Ministry of Foreign Affairs; www.diplomatie.gouv.fr/en) and click 'Coming to France'. Visas are not required for EU nationals or citizens of Iceland, Norway and Switzerland, and are required only for stays greater than 90 days for citizens of Australia, the USA, Canada, Hong Kong, Israel, Japan, Malaysia, New Zealand, Singapore, South Korea and many Latin American countries.

Language

The sounds used in spoken French can almost all be found in English. There are a couple of exceptions: nasal vowels (represented in our pronunciation guides by o or u followed by an almost inaudible nasal consonant sound m, n or ng), the 'funny' u (ew in our guides) and the deep-in-the-throat r. Bearing these few points in mind and reading our pronunciation guides below as if they were English, you'll be understood just fine.

BASICS

Hello.	*Bonjour.*	bon·zhoor
Goodbye.	*Au revoir.*	o·rer·vwa
Yes./No.	*Oui./Non.*	wee/non
Excuse me.	*Excusez-moi.*	ek·skew·zay·mwa
Sorry.	*Pardon.*	par·don
Please.	*S'il vous plaît.*	seel voo play
Thank you.	*Merci.*	mair·see

You're welcome.
De rien.　　　　der ree·en

Do you speak English?
Parlez-vous anglais?　　par·lay·voo ong·glay

I don't understand.
Je ne comprends pas.　　zher ner kom·pron pa

How much is this?
C'est combien?　　say kom·byun

ACCOMMODATION

Do you have any rooms available?
Est-ce que vous avez　　es·ker voo za·vay
des chambres libres?　　day shom·brer lee·brer

How much is it per night/person?
Quel est le prix　　kel ay ler pree
par nuit/personne?　　par nwee/per·son

DIRECTIONS

Can you show me (on the map)?
Pouvez-vous m'indiquer　　poo·vay·voo mun·dee·kay
(sur la carte)?　　(sewr la kart)

Where's ...?
Où est ...?　　oo ay ...

EATING & DRINKING

What would you recommend?
Qu'est-ce que vous　　kes·ker voo
conseillez?　　kon·say·yay

I'd like ..., please.
Je voudrais ...,　　zher voo·dray ...
s'il vous plaît.　　seel voo play

I'm a vegetarian.
Je suis végétarien/　　zher swee vay·zhay·ta·ryun/
végétarienne.　　vay·zhay·ta·ryen (m/f)

Please bring the bill.
Apportez-moi　　a·por·tay·mwa
l'addition,　　la·dee·syon
s'il vous plaît.　　seel voo play

EMERGENCIES

Help!
Au secours!　　o skoor

I'm lost.
Je suis perdu/perdue.　　zhe swee·pair·dew (m/f)

I'm ill.
Je suis malade.　　zher swee ma·lad

Want More?

For in-depth language information and handy phrases, check out Lonely Planet's *French Phrasebook*. You'll find it at **shop.lonelyplanet.com**, or you can buy Lonely Planet's iPhone phrasebooks at the Apple App Store.

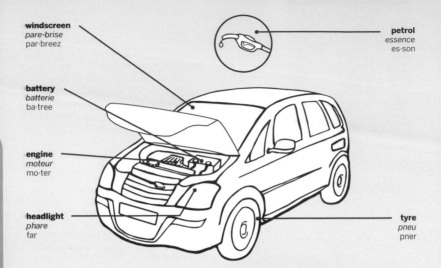

windscreen
pare-brise
par·breez

petrol
essence
es·son

battery
batterie
ba·tree

engine
moteur
mo·ter

headlight
phare
far

tyre
pneu
pner

Signs

Cédez la Priorité	Give Way
Sens Interdit	No Entry
Entrée	Entrance
Péage	Toll
Sens Unique	One Way
Sortie	Exit

Call the police!
Appelez la police! a·play la po·lees

Call a doctor!
Appelez un médecin! a·play un mayd·sun

ON THE ROAD

I'd like to hire a/an ...	*Je voudrais louer ...*	zher voo·dray loo·way ...
4WD	*un quatre-quatre*	un kat·kat
automatic/ manual	*une auto- matique/ manuel*	ewn o·to· ma·teek/ ma·nwel
motorbike	*une moto*	ewn mo·to

How much is it daily/weekly?
Quel est le tarif par jour/semaine? kel ay ler ta·reef par zhoor/ser·men

Does that include insurance?
Est-ce que l'assurance est comprise? es·ker la·sew·rons ay kom·preez

Does that include mileage?
Est-ce que le kilométrage est compris? es·ker ler kee·lo·may·trazh ay kom·pree

What's the speed limit?
Quelle est la vitesse maximale permise? kel ay la vee·tes mak·see·mal per·meez

Is this the road to ...?
C'est la route pour ...? say la root poor ...

Can I park here?
Est-ce que je peux stationner ici? es·ker zher per sta·syo·nay ee·see

Where's a service station?
Où est-ce qu'il y a une station-service? oo es·keel ya ewn sta·syon·ser·vees

Please fill it up.
Le plein, s'il vous plaît. ler plun seel voo play

I'd like (20) litres.
Je voudrais (vingt) litres. zher voo·dray (vung) lee·trer

Please check the oil/water.
Contrôlez l'huile/l'eau, s'il vous plaît. kon·tro·lay lweel/lo seel voo play

I need a mechanic.
J'ai besoin d'un mécanicien. zhay ber·zwun dun may·ka·nee·syun

The car/motorbike has broken down.
La voiture/moto est tombée en panne. la vwa·tewr/mo·to ay tom·bay on pan

I had an accident.
J'ai eu un accident. zhay ew un ak·see·don

BEHIND THE SCENES

SEND US YOUR FEEDBACK

We love to hear from travellers – your comments help make our books better. We read every word, and we guarantee that your feedback goes straight to the authors. Visit **lonelyplanet. com/contact** to submit your updates and suggestions.

Note: We may edit, reproduce and incorporate your comments in Lonely Planet products such as guidebooks, websites and digital products, so let us know if you don't want your comments reproduced or your name acknowledged. For a copy of our privacy policy visit lonelyplanet.com/privacy.

ACKNOWLEDGMENTS

Climate map data adapted from Peel MC, Finlayson BL & McMahon TA (2007) 'Updated World Map of the Köppen-Geiger Climate Classification', *Hydrology and Earth System Sciences*, 11, 163344.

Cover photographs: (front) Citroën 2CV, Provence–Alpes–Côte d'Azur, Eric Beracassat/4Corne; (back) Lavender field, Martina Meglic/Getty

THIS BOOK

This 1st edition of *Provence & Southeast France Road Trips* was researched and written by Oliver Berry, Gregor Clark, Emilie Filou, Donna Wheeler and Nicola Williams.This guidebook was produced by the following:

Product Editors Anne Mason, Luna Soo

Senior Cartographer Valentina Kremenchutskaya

Book Designers Katherine Marsh, Virginia Moreno

Assisting Editors Kate Evans, Andi Jones, Katie O'Connell

Cover Researcher Brendan Dempsey

Thanks to Shahara Ahmed, Sasha Baskett, James Hardy, Campbell McKenzie, Darren O'Connell, Martine Power, Tony Wheeler

OUR STORY

A beat-up old car, a few dollars in the pocket and a sense of adventure. In 1972 that's all Tony and Maureen Wheeler needed for the trip of a lifetime – across Europe and Asia overland to Australia. It took several months, and at the end – broke but inspired – they sat at their kitchen table writing and stapling together their first travel guide, *Across Asia on the Cheap*. Within a week they'd sold 1500 copies. Lonely Planet was born.

Today, Lonely Planet has offices in Melbourne, London and Oakland, with more than 600 staff and writers. We share Tony's belief that 'a great guidebook should do three things: inform, educate and amuse'.

INDEX

000 Map pages

NICOLA WILLIAMS

Originally from Britain, I've lived in France for over a decade. From my hillside house on the southern shore of Lake Geneva, it's a quick and easy motor to the Alps (call me a ski fiend...), Paris (art buff...), southern France (foodie...). I blog at tripalong.wordpress.com and tweet @Tripalong.

Read more about Nicola at: www.lonelyplanet.com/members/nicolawilliams

OUR WRITERS

OLIVER BERRY

My first trip to France was a family holiday to Provence at the age of two, and I've been back many times since while working on Lonely Planet's bestselling *France* guide. I've covered nearly every corner of L'Hexagone on my travels, but I have an especially soft spot for Corsica and the Pyrenees. When not in France, I can usually be found wandering the beaches and clifftops of my home county, Cornwall. I'm also a regular contributor to many other websites, newspapers and magazines, including *Lonely Planet Traveller*. Check out my latest travels at www.oliverberry.com.

Read more about Oliver at: www.lonelyplanet.com/ members/oliverberry

GREGOR CLARK

My first epic French road trip came on Bastille Day at age 20. Nearly broke and hitchhiking towards my next fruit-picking job, I landed a lift from a lost tourist and proceeded to spend the night winding through the fireworks-lit streets of every little village in Haute-Provence. To this day, I love nothing better than wandering France's back roads in search of hidden villages and unexpected treasures. I contribute regularly to Lonely Planet's European and South American guidebooks.

Read more about Gregor at: www.lonelyplanet. com/members/gregorclark

EMILIE FILOU

Emilie was born in Paris but spent most of her childhood holidays roaming the south of France. She now lives in London, where she works as a freelance journalist specialising in development issues in Africa. She goes to the Côte d'Azur every summer. See more of Emilie's work on www.emiliefilou.com; she tweets at @emiliefilou.

Read more about Emilie at: www.lonelyplanet.com/ members/emiliefilou

DONNA WHEELER

I've been visiting France for many years, but I really got to know the south when living just over the border in Turin. I'm the author of several Lonely Planet guidebooks and have published elsewhere on art, architecture and design, history and food. I'm also a creative consultant and travel experience planner. My Australian childhood was one epic coastal road trip, hunting down the best swimming spots and seafood dinners – something that stood me in good stead for this assignment.

Read more about Donna at: www.lonelyplanet. com/members/donnawheeler

3 1969 02536 8282

◀ MORE WRITERS

Published by Lonely Planet Publications Pty Ltd
ABN 36 005 607 983
1st edition – June 2015
ISBN 978 1 74360 708 4
© Lonely Planet 2015   Photographs © as indicated 2015
10 9 8 7 6 5 4 3 2 1
Printed in China